THE 1953 ESSEX FLOOD DISASTER

THE PEOPLE'S STORY

THE 1953 ESSEX FLOOD DISASTER

THE PEOPLE'S STORY

PATRICIA RENNOLDSON SMITH

The
History
Press

In memory of Peggy.

First published 2012
Reprinted 2012

The History Press
The Mill, Brimscombe Port
Stroud, Gloucestershire, GL5 2QG
www.thehistorypress.co.uk

© Patricia Rennoldson Smith, 2012

British Library Cataloguing in Publication Data.
A catalogue record for this book is available from the British Library.

ISBN 978 0 7524 6541 8

Typesetting and origination by The History Press
Printed and bound in Great Britain by
Marston Book Services Limited, Didcot

CONTENTS

	Acknowledgements	6
	Introduction	7
1.	Harwich	9
2.	Wrabness, Mistley and Manningtree	24
3.	Bramble Island	26
4.	Clacton and Walton-on-the-Naze	30
5.	Jaywick	31
6.	St Osyth and Point Clear	50
7.	Brightlingsea	58
8.	Wivenhoe	60
9.	Mersea Island	62
10.	Tollesbury	65
11.	Heybridge and Maldon	67
12.	Bradwell	70
13.	Althorne and Hockley	76
14.	Burnham-on-Crouch, Foulness and Havengore	78
15.	Wallasea and Creeksea	90
16.	Great Wakering	95
17.	Southend-on-Sea and Leigh-on-Sea	103
18.	Canvey Island and Benfleet	106
19.	Tilbury	133
	Will it Ever Happen Again?	136
	Recorded Deaths Due to the Flood in Essex	138
	About the Author	141
	Bibliography	142

ACKNOWLEDGEMENTS

First, thanks to the people of Essex, who have made this book possible by telling me their experiences during that dreadful time; you may not find your name in the text, but you are part of the story, so thank you! My life has been enriched by meeting you, by learning more about Essex history, and by discovering the fascinating secret parts of Essex where I found you.

To everyone who kindly supplied photographs for the book, please accept the accreditation as my grateful thanks.

For draft checking and advice on specific areas, special thanks to Ray Plummer of the Guild Hall, Harwich; Peter Wright of Jaywick; Sean O'Dell of St Osyth; Margaret Stone of Brightlingsea; Kevin Bruce of Bradwell; John Threadgold of Great Wakering; and Graham Stevens of Canvey Island.

For their assistance, advice and encouragement, my thanks to Anne Kemp-Luck at the Guild Hall, Harwich; Brenda Dixson and Brenda Oliver of Jaywick; Peter Gant and John Rowland of the Manningtree Museum; Nick Lee and Phyllis Hendy of St Osyth; Robert Shotton of Brightlingsea; my friend Pearl Perriman of Barling; and Mark and Rosemary Roberts of Paglesham.

To Janet Penn and Councillor Ray Howard, both of Canvey Island; Nicola Pontius and the staff of Canvey Library; and Martin Canter for the Quaker records.

To Bob Crump of Foulness Heritage Centre and the people of Foulness; Becky Wash of the Essex Police Museum; James Melley of BBC Essex; Peter Edwards of the RNLI; Ken Crowe of Southend Museum; Stephen Nunn of Maldon; the staff of the Essex Record Office; and Patrick John of Rochford.

Many thanks to my friend Margaret Hurst for draft reading and typing.

Finally, to my wonderful family, my husband Brian, and to Lesley, Alan, Rob, Nadine and sister Margaret for checking, advising, typing and listening to my endless flood talk.

INTRODUCTION

Several books have been written about the 1953 flood but this is the first to capture the impact on the people affected. The story is told through the memories of those caught in the disaster.

Hilda Grieve's *The Great Tide*, published by Essex County Council in 1959, was the first account of the Essex flood. It is still the default reference work for students of the event and I give thanks for the availability of that excellent work. My friend Peggy lost her husband and young son in the Canvey flood and though part of her story appears in *The Great Tide*, Peggy did not speak of the tragedy for almost thirty years. Hers was one of the many heartrending accounts of survivors recounted to me. Young at the time and now elderly, their memories are fresh, vivid and searing, yet they have delighted me with their generosity and entertained me with their down-to-earth good humour. Their wish is that their memories are recorded as part of the nation's story.

Over the centuries, the low-lying coastal areas of Essex have frequently suffered flooding. But by 1953, large-scale residential development on marshland resulted in thousands more people being at risk, especially since many dwellings were of a type and construction least likely to withstand the surge. On that fateful afternoon, tide watchers along the coast noted the weak ebb – a sure sign of trouble – but nobody anticipated how high the next incoming tide would be. That night the North Sea surged in a fury over and through the sea walls. There was no central flood warning system, and the early loss of phone lines halted the passage of messages down the coast. More fortunate residents were alerted when seawater burst through their doors as they slept, or when neighbours shouted above the storm. Those not so lucky slept on towards death.

Saturday, 31 January 1953 was the night of a spring tide, but long before high water, a deep atmospheric low pressure system above Scotland raised the water levels. When the water entered the North Sea, a gale-force northerly wind whipped up and increased the height of the swell, resulting in a wall of water being driven south. As it funnelled into the bottleneck between England and Holland, this North Sea tsunami reached a height of at least 10 feet above the expected height of the spring tide. The rotation of the earth then deflected the water towards the British Isles.

The violent surge swept down the east coasts of Scotland and England and up the eastern river estuaries, causing havoc in its wake. Martin Golledge, a police officer in

Chelsea, saw water lapping over the Thames embankment fifty minutes before high tide. London was saved from serious flooding when sea walls were breached on Canvey and floodwater released into Essex.

The county had been 'on standby' throughout the war years and immediately leapt into 'blitz' mode. Families left their flooded homes, often with nothing more than the clothes they stood up in. False teeth, spectacles and babies' bottles were left behind, but in a few hours, particularly between midnight and 2 a.m., relief was organised: the schools opened, staff and helpers were in position, and warmth, food and clothing provided. The Harwich Town Clerk later wrote, 'It is a privilege to pay a tribute to the other chief officers for their patience, fortitude and powers of organisation and improvisation in adversity, and to the other officers and employees for all their hard work and unfailing keenness at all times since the flood'.

The Essex Coroner said that with so many people involved it was nothing short of a miracle that there were not more deaths, but the miracle was achieved by the tireless work of organisations such as the police, fire brigade and ambulance services. Countless volunteers also donated their time and energy to work long, hard hours in dreadful conditions to alleviate the suffering. Some groups are mentioned in the text. Any omissions are unintentional – all are deserving of praise.

The 1953 flood was the worst peacetime disaster ever to strike Britain. One hundred and twenty people died in Essex as a direct result, and other lives were shortened by the trauma. Many survivors and rescuers will bear the scars of what they witnessed for the rest of their lives. Official reports, written at the time, however, record the selflessness and stoicism of the people. In the midst of the catastrophe which befell them, residents from Harwich to Tilbury acted on their own initiative and spontaneously worked for the good of all.

This is their story.

Patricia Rennoldson Smith, 2012

AUTHOR'S NOTE
I have made every effort to trace copyright and apologise to anyone I may have inadvertently missed. I can assure you this is an error on my behalf and can be rectified by the publishers if you would care to get in touch.

1

HARWICH

The sea is a close neighbour to the people of Harwich. They know all her moods, are prepared for the unexpected, and accept what she throws at them. But on Saturday, 31 January 1953, a gale-force, screeching wind battered the shore all day, and the hardy Harwich folk, still up and about in the evening, looked anxiously at the rising tide.

The town of Harwich lies on a narrow peninsula jutting out into the mouth of the River Stour and looking towards Shotley in Suffolk. It is the northernmost point of the Essex coast.

The old town, with its many ancient pubs and fine Georgian and Victorian houses, experienced flooding on the night of 31 January, but it was the Bathside area which bore the brunt of the onslaught. Bathside was protected from direct attack from the sea by a clay bank, and between the bank and the residential streets there was a muddy marsh basin, where locals kept their chickens and pigs.

The spring high tide was predicted for 12.52 a.m. that night, with a height of 5.6 feet. But when Mr Waters, the Harbourmaster, checked the height of the water at the quay at 9.20 p.m., he was concerned enough to go immediately to the police station to report that the tide would be exceptionally high. When he returned to the quay at 10 p.m. the water was up to the top of the wall; 4 feet above the expected level, with more than two hours to go until high tide. The police were not unduly concerned but they informed the Harwich fire brigade and, following normal procedure, warned the Clacton police, who, at 10.13 p.m., alerted Chelmsford. Chelmsford immediately advised New Scotland Yard.

At about 10.40 p.m. fisherman Carter, becoming concerned about the strong winds, set out from his home in Alexandra Road to secure the boat he kept moored at Gas House Creek, but at the sea wall he realised he would not make it to the creek and rushed home, warning neighbours as he went.

By 11 p.m. waves were pounding the sea wall at Bathside and breaking over it. The wall was holding, but water was flowing across the mud towards the animal huts. The police had begun warning residents, some of whom replied that they'd 'seen it all before – nothing to worry about'.

But half an hour later most of Harwich was under water and worse was yet to come. Just after midnight a second great wave burst over the sea wall. The wall gave way, and

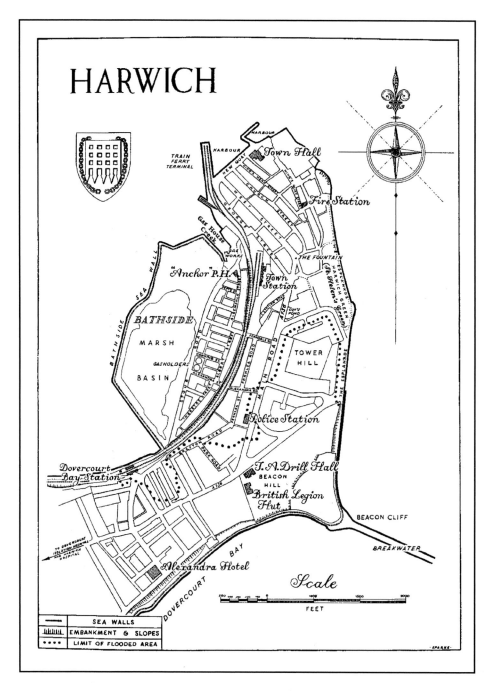

A map of Harwich in 1953. (Reproduced from the 1953 Ordnance
Survey Map courtesy of Essex Record Office)

a tidal wave stormed across Stour Road into Bathside. The shock to the residents was incalculable, and not all would survive.

The home of Mrs Brennan in Ingestre Street was the first house in the track of the wave. She heard a noise like an explosion; the house shuddered as the windows and the front door burst in with a torrent of icy water. Though sturdily built of brick, the walls of two houses in Alexandra Road were demolished that night and the party wall of two adjoining houses in Kings Head Street collapsed.

At 11.30 there was no water in Alexandra Road, but Carter, after alerting his wife to the danger, went to warn a neighbour whose children slept in the basement. Minutes later he heard his wife scream and saw water pouring down the street. He ran for the safety of his home just as floodwater burst into the front and back doors simultaneously.

Fisherman Carter was one of the residents of Harwich who recorded memories of that night. He wrote, 'I decided to leave the house as I was afraid it might collapse. I carried one of my children to dry ground through about 2 feet of water. (Carrying) the second child it topped my thigh boots and then with my wife on my shoulders getting her feet wet. My height is approximately 6 foot. I went back for the dog and had to swim both ways. All this happened in five to ten minutes.'

Alexandra Road from the level crossing. Note the water mark on the wall. (Courtesy of Harwich Town Council)

Miss Harrington and her sister were warned by Mr Carter that the wall had given way, and fifteen minutes later the force of the rushing water broke open the back door. By twelve o'clock the ground floor was flooded and there was 18 inches of water upstairs. Here they huddled, cold and wet, until daybreak, when, looking out of their window, they saw in the road 'all kinds of little boats and amongst them hampering their progress – dead chickens, debris and swimming pigs'.

Mr Pearl Lofts and his wife, Elsie, managed the Anchor Hotel on the corner of Stour Road and Albemarle Street in Bathside, close to Gas House Creek. Mr Lofts, recognising the danger signs, went with his wife into the cellar to secure the beer barrels at about 11.30 p.m. Mrs Lofts recalled that half an hour later she heard a noise from outside and water started to flow into the cellar. Pearl took her hand and said, 'Come on Else,' and then she was washed away from him. The water came in through the outside cellar door so fast that Elsie was swept up the cellar steps and out through the door in seconds. Pressure of the rising water then slammed the door shut and made it impossible for her husband to get out. Mrs Lofts remembered 'being up there, but there was no stairs, just water up to the ceiling'.

The water was approximately 14 feet deep in the cellar and though many attempts were made, Mr Lofts' body could not be recovered until Tuesday afternoon, when police broke through the floor above the still-flooded cellar.

The Anchor Hotel, Bathside, where Mr Lofts drowned in the cellar. (Courtesy of Harwich Town Council)

The Bruce family home, where three people died in 1953. (Author's collection)

Just a short distance away, another tragic story was unfolding involving 68-year-old Walter Mallows, of Vansittart Street, a would-be rescuer, and the Bruce family, who lived round the corner at No. 15 Albert Street. The Bruce's home, a ground floor council flat, was 3 feet below street level. The door was on the side, the upper flat being accessed by a door and stairs at the front.

Mr and Mrs Bruce went to bed in the room at the front at 10.30 p.m., but about an hour later were woken by what they thought was heavy rain hitting the windowpane. Mr Bruce looked out of the window and saw a torrent of water pouring through the front gate, down the step and encircling the front of the flats. They quickly dressed. Mr Bruce later recalled that he, 'Went to the kiddie's room, picked up Richard, opened the side door and took him round the front of the building and up to the flat above, where I left him. The water was then around my knees. I went back down to the flat to get Janet out of bed.' There, his wife was waiting in waist-high water, holding baby Pauline. Each carrying a child, they fought their way through the water to the side entrance, but when the door was flung open, Mrs Bruce became terrified by the sight of water surging along the narrow side passage. She could not move. Trying to encourage her, Mr Bruce stepped out into a torrent of turbulent water up to his neck, and, still desperately clutching Janet, was swept helplessly towards the railway embankment behind the flats. He lost sight of his wife and baby daughter – and never saw them again.

Between the back of the flats and the railway line, floodwater was trapped, and at least 7 feet deep, but father and child survived.

Unfortunately, Mrs Bruce did not. PC Harold King was on duty that night and at 12.15 was outside No. 15 Albert Street. There, in the front window of the Bruce's flat, he saw a man he knew. The man was Walter Mallows. At about 11.30 that evening Mr Mallows had told his son that there would be flooding and that he would go and help anybody who needed it. He headed for Albert Street.

The police constable later stated that he could see quite plainly the three people in the room. Mr Mallows was kneeling on the windowsill with his head partly out of the small fanlight window. He called out, 'Sergeant get us out. There is a young woman in here with a small child.' The woman was standing by his side at the window, holding the child in her arms, in approximately 4 foot of water. The police constable later explained what happened next:

' I at once tried to reach these trapped persons but the swirling and cascading floodwaters and the steep slope leading to the flats from Albert Street made this quite impossible for me. The water was so strong and was rising rapidly. I appealed to the occupants of the upstairs flats to lower sheets or a rope and enquired of several persons where I could locate a boat but unfortunately no boat could be obtained.

The water by this time was 5ft deep at road level and, having assured myself that I could do no more to save these unfortunate people, I battled my way against the swirling waters and debris to a level crossing at Ferndale Road, where I saw the water cascading over the railway lines towards Fernlea Road. I made my way along the railway lines to the rear of those flats but could see no person about. The swirling waters made it impossible for me to enter the flats via their rear garden. '

Later that morning, fireman William Walpole was part of the crew of a rowing boat manned by a Petty Officer and two boys from HMS *Ganges* (the Royal Navy training ship at Shotley). Passing No. 15 Albert Street, he saw the body of a man hanging head and arms downward from a ground floor window. The water was level with his hands. He was apparently dead. The man was later identified as Mr Mallows. The men eased the body out of the window and took it to Stour Street, where a Special Constable was collecting the dead.

PC Finch was on duty in Harwich, assisting in the recovery of the bodies of flood victims on Monday, 2 February and, at 2 p.m., he reached the Bruce's flat. The water was still halfway up the wall and the police officer was forced to climb in the front room window. There he found the bodies of Mrs Bruce and her 16-month-old daughter, Pauline. He noted that the water level had reached approximately 6 inches from the ceiling.

Mr Aynsley was fortunate in being woken by a rat-atat-tat on the door of his home in Grafton Road, Dovercourt. Like his neighbour, fisherman Carter, Mr Aynsley

'I'm not catching many fish!' (Artwork by Mike Maynard)

recorded what happened: 'I got up and, looking out of the window, saw a dark figure hurrying up the street. I shouted after him and he yelled back in the teeth of the gale something unintelligible, but I heard the words "sea wall". I found that the back of the house, which backed onto the embankment, was flooded to about 3 foot while the front, which is higher, was dry. With the coming of the dawn, looking out of the front window, I saw water rolling up the street almost like the Seven Bore. We could hear the screams of those trapped in Bathside, but were powerless to help'. The clocks in Bathside had stopped at 12.20 a.m.

Mr Aynsley added, 'The view from the back window was even worse. Where normally we saw the railway embankment, a road, and beyond that the sea wall, and then the river; now, there was nothing but water from our house right over to the Suffolk side, just an odd tree top sticking out. A scene of devastation.' The water eventually rose to 6 foot at the back of the house and 14 foot at the front. Down the road, a boy was hanging out of a bedroom window with a piece of string and a bent pin on a stick, shouting to all and sundry that he wasn't catching many fish.

Until this time the 6-foot high railway embankment had formed a barrier protecting the rest of Harwich from the floodwater. No one imagined the bank would be overtopped. Most people on the other side were asleep, unaware of any danger; but the speed, height and force of the surge took all in its path.

In Fernlea Road, immediately behind the railway, Mr and Mrs Byatt were awoken by a tremendous roaring noise, caused when the water crashed over the railway embankment into the depression between the railway and the main road. This turbulent maelstrom joined the water surging from the north, east, and west. It was assumed that the level would drop when the tide ebbed, but at 1 a.m. floodwater was trapped in two pockets, and Harwich was in darkness.

Those who could escape made their way, wet through in their bed clothes, to the police station. One man rushed in with a chicken under one arm and a rabbit under the other. 'Where shall I put these?' He was told to put them in the basement, but after a short time the basement and ground floor were flooded and the animals had to be moved. The water in the police station eventually rose to a height of 7 feet, and the officers had to leave the station via a window into a boat, to carry out their operational duties.

Rear of Fernlea Road. Note the flood mark above the window. (Courtesy of Harwich Town Council)

Harwich was flooded from The Quay to the junction of Main Road and Barrack Lane. No rail service operated between Harwich Town and Parkston Quay stations until 24 February, as railway lines were washed away and the three local stations were flooded. The floodwater in Dovercourt reached as far as The Drive and Hall Lane. In Parkston, 150 homes were flooded to a depth of between 1 and 7 feet, and the flood spread to cover the marshes and fields below Oakley.

Mrs Winchester and her husband, the Harwich Town stationmaster, went to a dinner and dance at Parkston Quay that night. When they left the hall they were amazed to find floodwater up to their knees, and were forced to shelter at a friend's house until the tide turned. Mrs Winchester later recorded:

‘ We set forth with a torch towards Harwich Station in knee-deep water. The holes where the ballast had been washed away and the debris piled up made it a nightmare journey. Suddenly one of my husband's legs went into a hole under the water, wire became entangled round his leg and he lost his footing. After an endless time I managed to get him free of it and on we went. There were dogs, chickens, cats and pigs carried with the tide, some dead, some alive. The pigs were swimming well until caught up in debris. Their shrieks I shall always hear. Suddenly, a convoy of coffins surrounded us, from the undertaker's yard beside the railway line. We'd stood still a few moments, to rest and regain breath and my husband decided that if we got into a coffin we might push ourselves along. I strongly opposed the idea. But then my leg went down a hole and I was dragged away from my husband. I went so quickly! No doubt it was the tide. After a time he managed to get me up and a short rest ensued. Then I hung onto a coffin for dear life.

How thankful we were to see the Harwich signal box. The water was much deeper there and I was glad to be helped up the steps. I couldn't speak for several minutes but I heard Foreman Cooper, a grand old Suffolk man, exclaim 'Where the devil ha yar bin too together? I've bin round and round yar house a knockin and a bangin, nobody answered, only tha ode dawg a barkin'. I found later that Cooper had fallen into the water and it had shaken him considerably. I was told there was 5 feet of water between the box and my home, and there I had to stay.

As dawn broke we saw six Trinity House men struggling along the line with water up to their waists. They told us they must get to Trinity House and get the boats out to rescue people. From another direction, the fishermen were lifting boats over the debris to be near when it became sufficiently light to commence rescue work, and the boys from the Ganges Naval School were doing likewise. Their efforts were almost superhuman. ’

Mrs Winchester was taken to the home of train guard, Mr English, in Dovercourt. 'What comfort to change my clothes and sit in an armchair by the fire with a cup of tea.'

'Get into a coffin? No thank you!' (Artwork by Mike Maynard)

Mr Winchester set off to arrange bus transport while the train track was under water, and returned with Mr English at about 7.30 p.m., 'hungry, tired and covered with mud, but content in mind that in spite of all difficulties transport was still maintained'.

Help began to arrive very early on Sunday, 1 February, when fifty boys from HMS *Ganges* and a Petty Officer brought their sailing dinghies and small boats to Harwich. Once there, floating debris made it almost impossible for the crews to row. Many streets were completely blocked. The boys waded through the water, which was sometimes up to their shoulders and always up to their waists, pushing the boats to rescue stranded families. Years later, people still spoke of the 'wonderful Naval boys from Shotley, wading up to their waists to get near'.

It was extremely difficult to get boats near enough to the houses to begin the rescue. Sea Scout Goswell of the 4th Dovercourt Sea Scouts, along with his colleagues, answered the call for volunteers and all available dinghies to help evacuate people in Harwich. Later he described how 'Old people had to be persuaded to leave their bedroom windows and crawl down the wet and slippery overhanging eaves of the lower window, into a rocking boat. One man would support the evacuee and one the boat'. Some of the boats needed to be bailed out and chamber pots were handed from windows for the purpose. Through a window into the Aynsley house, they saw that the table, which had been laid for breakfast, had floated almost up to the ceiling. When Mrs Aynsley returned to her otherwise ruined home, she found that the table had settled down again 'with all the china and cutlery in perfect order'.

By dawn the rescue mission had begun in earnest. Search parties were quickly organised, each official group composed of representatives from the police, fire brigade and military personnel. The navy, local fishermen and any able-bodied person, young or old, took to the boats. 'Many took parts of their clothes off and swam to the people's aid.' Sea Scout Goswell mentioned that his friend, Tom Bell, dived into the cold and fast-flowing water to retrieve a ladder to help in rescue operations. There were a number of instances of police and firemen having to leave their vehicles and swim to save their own lives.

In McDough Cottages, where 7-year-old Cleoni Hill lived with her family, the water reached the upper windows. The cottages, tucked in between Station and Ferndale Roads, were the first to feel the effects of the floodwater coming in from Dovercourt Bay, when, at 11.45 p.m., the back door burst open, bringing the dustbin in with the fast-flowing water. The terrified family reached the upper floor and were horrified to see the mattresses floating. Some hours later when rescue came, as Cleoni stepped out of the window into a boat, she was pitched into the deep, cold and dirty water when her aunt accidently unbalanced the boat. Luckily, she was a good swimmer.

There were many brave and selfless actions that night. A young lad was seen rescuing a mother with her newborn baby from her flat in Albert Street, by floating their mattress out of the window then swimming with it, helped by her husband and another man, until they reached dry ground. But four more people, sleeping downstairs due to illness, were trapped by the floodwater between the railway line and the Main Road and died in their beds that night.

Stanley Vincent, a retired Trinity House Lighthouse Master was bedridden, suffering from inoperable cancer, when his house in Grafton Road was flooded. His wife woke in the upstairs bedroom to take him his 1.45 a.m. medication and found floodwater up to the top of the stairs. Her husband, sleeping downstairs, was sedated and must have died immediately. His bed was submerged. There was still 5 foot of water in the house when his body was removed on 2 February.

Edward Ellis had suffered two strokes just before Christmas 1952, and, as a result, was bedridden and sleeping in the downstairs front room of his house in Fernlea Road. His wife slept with him so as to be on hand if he should need her. About midnight, Mrs Ellis heard the sound of rushing water. When she got out of bed to investigate, she found about 1 foot of water in the room. She opened the front door to discover the cause and a wall of water knocked her over. Struggling to her feet, she shouted for help but her attempts were futile. The body of her husband was recovered about noon on Monday.

The daughter-in-law of Mr and Mrs Shipley had tea with the couple at their home in Station Road on Saturday afternoon. They were both well and in their normal good spirits. However, her father-in-law was suffering from a minor illness, so man and wife slept in a downstairs room that night. Their next-door neighbour, who was escaping the floodwater in her house by climbing over her back wall into the railway station yard with her young grandchildren, heard Mrs Shipley screaming for help. There was nothing she could do as the water had risen to a depth of 8 feet. Mrs Shipley had full use of just one of her arms and was trapped by the bedclothes. The couple died together in their bed. There was 5 feet of water in the room when their bodies were recovered the next day. They were taken to the Empire Cinema, Dovercourt – a temporary mortuary.

Meanwhile, for those who survived, a well-organised rest centre had been set up with utmost speed and efficiency. The Harwich Town Clerk telephoned Miss Weston of the Women's Voluntary Service (WVS), at 3 a.m. on Sunday morning, and by 3.30 a.m. twelve volunteers had reported for duty and the Territorial Drill Hall was ready for action.

The Ganges Boys to the rescue. (Courtesy of Essex Police Museum)

Albert Street after the flood. (Courtesy of Harwich Town Council)

Victims poured in, shocked, wet, cold, often badly cut and frightened. Names were given to the police, while the Red Cross and St John Ambulance nurses attended to injuries, and the Co-op provided food, tea and milk. The Salvation Army and the WVS kept the organisation running smoothly. Wet clothes were washed and hung up to dry. One member had brought along her mangle – and her husband to turn the wheel!

Scout troops had been enlisted to assist, and in Harwich three cubs of the first Dovercourt Troop (boys under 11) presented themselves at the police station on the morning of Monday, 2 February, asking whether they could help. They were beautifully turned out in their uniforms and did a good job of work. They were sent to the rest centre, where David Branch and Melvyn Topple acted as messengers, and Roger Hawkins was a guide to an ambulance driver.

By midday on Sunday the hall was full, and owing to the depth of the water in some streets, not everyone could be rescued, so boats took tea and food to the trapped victims, one of whom later said, 'The sound of the mobile's horn was music to the ear'.

Flood relief donations arrived from across the country and from abroad. Canada sent carpets, Ethiopia sent coffee, children from Kuwait sent toys, a school in Blackpool collected £10 for the children of Canvey, and pictured is one of the twenty houses Norway sent to Harwich. (Author's collection)

One distressed survivor. (Artwork by Mike Maynard)

One survivor made a weary rescuer smile. Two days after the surge, a fireman found a parrot in an abandoned, flooded house. He placed the cage on the bow of the rescue boat and began to row to dry land. The parrot hopped backwards and forwards along his perch, gazing anxiously at the seething water on each side and squawking, 'Oh my gawd! Oh my gawd!'

2

WRABNESS, MISTLEY AND MANNINGTREE

Between 11 p.m. and midnight the incoming tide surged up the Stour estuary, earlier and higher than expected, causing serious flooding in Wrabness, Mistley and Manningtree. At Shore Farm in Wrabness, the farmer and his wife were woken by a neighbour at 11.30 p.m. and within ten minutes, in knee-deep water, they had moved their horses and pigs to safety, from a shed near the sea wall, but returning for the mare and her two foals found the gate completely under water. A Suffolk horse, ridden into the water in an attempt to open the gate, shied and refused to go further, but a braver Suffolk 'breasted its way through to the gate, which was opened, and the mare was driven out, with the two foals, their heads just above the water, following her'.

At Mistley, the constable on duty was leaving the police station at 11.45 p.m., when a passer-by told him the water had started to flow over the road at Mistley Walls. It was not unusual at that time of year for a little water to cover the B1352 at high tide, but as high water was not due until 1.36 a.m., and a strong north-west wind was blowing, the constable went to investigate and found the road impassable. The kiln at Edme Ltd, producers of malted cereals, had been extinguished by the flood water, and employees were out waking householders.

At nearby Portishead House (an ex-vicarge owned in 1953 by Brooks (Mistley)) – maltsters and corn merchants – for its workers to live in), a foreman for the company, who was asleep on a couch in the kitchen, reported how he 'was woken up by a curious noise, put his hand down to find his torch and put it right into the water'. The time was approximately one o'clock. He found that the water was rising very quickly, and before long the whole couch was afloat and water was shooting up the sink waste 'like a fountain', nearly hitting the ceiling. Outside it was halfway up the window pane. With difficulty, he forced open the door leading to the stairs, but the flow of water knocked him down and the floating furniture hampered his recovery. Eventually he got up the stairs to safety. His dog was stranded for another hour or more in the water before it could be rescued. The pendulum clock was stopped by water at 1.30 a.m.

The foreman kept several sows and pigs at Portishead House. Most were drowned but one little pig escaped and, wet, frightened and alone, found its way in the dark, up the hill to the Mistley police station, a journey of half a mile. On arrival 'it was taken into custody'.

In Manningtree, the sea walls were overtopped by successive waves, increasing in height. Then, lashed by the wind, water beat at the wall from back and front till it crumbled; the water covering the Lawford Hall marshes to a depth of 3 to 4 feet, and reaching as far back as the Skinners Arms public house in Station Road. Floodwater reached the upper floor of Mr and Mrs Head's house in Station Road. The couple were rescued and stayed at one of the local almshouses until their home was clean and dry.

This little pig survived. (Reuter's image, reproduced courtesy of Essex Record Office)

3

BRAMBLE ISLAND

On the night of the flood, at the Explosives and Chemical Products factory on Bramble Island, near Great Oakley, 68-year-old nightwatchman Henry Archibald was alone on the otherwise uninhabited and bleak outpost. He knew nothing of the expected abnormally high tide that night and had no neighbour to warn him. Suddenly, just before midnight, the sea crashed into his office and within seconds floodwater was up to his knees and rapidly rising. He attempted, without success, to report the situation to the works manager, Dr Baldwin, by telephone. Eventually, Dr Baldwin managed to get through to him. They spoke hurriedly into the crackling line. Above the background noise of the flooding tide, Dr Baldwin told the trapped worker to make for safety on high ground immediately. Soon afterwards, the telephone and lights failed and Henry Archibald was never heard from again.

Dr Baldwin drove towards the factory to relieve the nightwatchman, but the level and speed of the water made it impossible to reach Bramble Island from any direction. (Bramble Island is actually a peninsula: an area of reclaimed marshland surrounded by a sea wall on three sides and a counter wall on the other.) Dr Baldwin then drove to Great Oakley and woke PC Ernest Cuthbert, the village constable, who, hoping the nightwatchman had managed to leave the factory, set out to search the route between the flooded island and his home in Little Oakley. Failing to find him, the constable and the works manager went to Dovercourt, woke lorry driver Leonard Gosling, and asked him to help in the search.

Mr Gosling collected a friend, Donald Harris, and loaded a boat onto a lorry. At 3 a.m. they set out for Bramble Island, where the boat was launched in the dark – and where, in places, the water was level with the telephone wires. Neither man knew the island well. These brave and determined individuals were soon surrounded by barrels of explosives, which crashed against the boat, making rowing difficult as well as dangerous. Before long, the boat was abandoned and the men battled forward on foot. With icy water sometimes up to their necks, they clawed their way slowly around the ruined factory buildings, calling out into the gale as they went, but they found no nightwatchman. When a fresh torrent of water crashed towards them, they turned back, exhausted.

The remains of factory buildings on Bramble Island. (Reproduced courtesy of Essex Record Office)

Henry Archibald, who died a lonely death on Bramble Island,
photographed with his wife Jane. (Courtesy of Fraser Morrison)

At daybreak the next morning the constable walked to the factory along the top of the counter wall with several employees, who had volunteered to search for their workmate. They did not find Henry Archibald, but they found his lamp lying in a dyke near the factory.

On 7 February, one week after the disappearance of Henry Archibald, a group of Territorial Army personnel – posted on the island after the flood to install searchlights – continued the search. They recorded floodwater marks on the wall of the derelict office, indicating a water level of 5 feet. Ominously, in the corner, still swinging in the breeze, hung the telephone with which Henry Archibald had tried to get help before being washed away in the flood.

Fraser Morrison, Henry's grandson, later told how his grandmother, knowing nothing of the futile searches being made on Bramble Island, prepared her husband's Sunday roast as usual. When time passed without his arrival, brothers and uncles joined the search, spending day after day walking the freezing marshes in search of him. They searched at first desperately, hoping to find him alive, and eventually hoping to find and bring home his body.

The nightwatchman's phone was in the corner, swinging in
the breeze … (Artwork by Mike Maynard)

Felixstowe beach, where Henry Archibald's body was washed up. (Library of
Congress, Prints & Photographs Division, LC-DIG-ppmsc-08373)

Henry Archibald's body was washed up on the beach at Felixstowe, Suffolk, two
months later and more than three miles away, at 11.30 a.m. on 5 April.

4

CLACTON AND WALTON-ON-THE-NAZE

The Naze sticks out into the North Sea, rather like the nose of a puppy, and the town of Walton, further south, is joined to its head by a thin neck, only 30 yards wide, behind which are the Walton Backwaters.

At 10 p.m. on Saturday 31st, the watchman at the Walton coastguard lookout recorded violent gusts of wind from the north-west, between 45 and 54mph. The sea was rough and with a very heavy swell. By 10.30, when he was sure that the tide would be unusually high, he telephoned the Royal National Lifeboat Institution (RNLI), and by 10.50 p.m. the sea was coming across the road in front of his lookout. Thirty minutes later, the water was up to the garden of the coastguard station and part of the front fence had been carried away in water 2 feet deep.

The night duty constable went to Saville and North Streets to advise those who could to seek safety upstairs. He was met with water 6 feet deep. Later, waves reported as high as 6-8 feet tore beach huts from their sites and washed them out to sea. The concrete promenade was smashed like matchwood, and iron railings were twisted like pieces of wire.

But it was from the backwaters that serious flooding would attack Walton, flowing stealthily across the acres of marshland into the streets of Walton at its narrowest point. The tide had overtopped, and in places breached the protecting walls.

That night, 194 Walton properties were flooded, but here water flowed out freely with the ebb tide, or could be pumped out of houses. Sixty people were initially made homeless, but most were able to return home within six days.

Further south, in Clacton, which sits higher on the shore, water merely lapped over the promenade. But Clacton police, fire brigade and all relevant organisations went to the assistance of their neighbour, Jaywick.

5

JAYWICK

A child haunted by the death of his beloved grandmother, Terry May's story is a tragic one:

' My life started very strangely and continued that way. Soon after I was born my parents split up and I went to live with my mother's parents in Jaywick, while my mother went to work in London. My grandparents had lived in London, in Acton, and had suffered night after night with the bombing during the Blitz. When their café was blown up they moved to Jaywick for a more peaceful existence, and that's how I came to be there in 1953. It's a nice place to live, but as it turned out it was anything but safe.

Ted Bangle's wife was swept away. He is pictured holding his grandson, Terry May. (Courtesy of Terry May)

On that night in 1953, I remember the water splashing against the window and I suppose that we all simultaneously woke up and got ourselves ready. My grandfather took the fateful decision to go into the water and try to escape from it, rather than going up into the attic, which in hindsight would have been wiser, because the water didn't go up that high. But in the middle of the night, when you've just woken up to disaster with the water screaming all around, who knows what is the best thing to do? My grandmother lifted me up onto my grandfather's back and said, 'You take the boy,' and they both said, 'Whatever you do, you must not let go'. I remember that! We opened the door, went into the water and that is the last I ever saw of my grandmother. It was pitch black, but we made our way up to Crossways and to Mr Stewart's in Union Way. How he managed to get up there with me on his back is truly incredible. The road wasn't tarmacked and there were big potholes. I was only 3 years old but I was heavy. He did really well to save both of us. **'**

The bungalow home of Mr and Mrs Bangle in Meadow Way was set back from the road, behind another chalet. The door was on the side. Terry's grandfather later told how, as they opened the door, his wife was swept off her feet in the strong current and carried away. 'I never saw her again'. With his terrified 3-year-old grandson on his back he pulled himself along, in utter darkness, in cold, fast-flowing water, through an alleyway between houses, where submerged gates, fences, barbed wire and potholes had to be negotiated before he even reached the unmade road to begin his journey. Mrs Helena Bangle's body was recovered two days later from the rear of the house next door. She was 62.

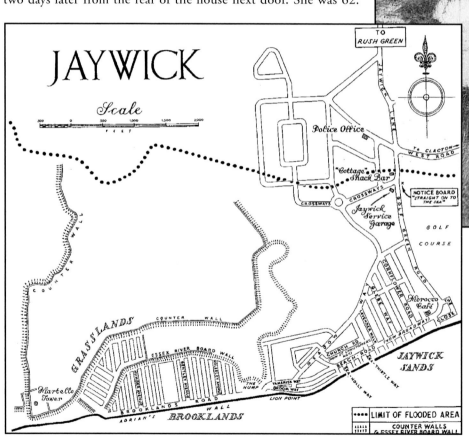

A map of Jaywick in 1953.
(Reproduced from the 1953 Ordnance Survey Map courtesy of Essex Record Office)

Shattered homes in Jaywick. (Courtesy of Essex Police Museum)

Terry's mother telephoned Clacton police from Shepherds Bush, London, to check on her parents and son as soon as she heard news of the flood. Terry continued:

‘ After the flood I went to live with my Aunty Flo, who was in her sixties. Then sometimes I lived with my mother in a flat. I was a very nervous child. The wind rushing round the flats reminded me of the night of the storm and I would shiver under the bedclothes.

My grandfather had nothing to do with us after the flood. I rarely saw him. I was a child and didn't know why. Young as I was I felt responsible for the loss of my beloved grandmother. If grandfather had not had to save me, he might have managed to save her. The flood broke my family up. Grandmother was the lynchpin who kept the family together. It fell apart after that night. ’

Jaywick is a holiday resort boasting a good stretch of sandy beach, approximately two miles west of Clacton. In 1953, it consisted mainly of small chalet-type bungalows, many built on concrete piers, some with lofts in the roof space, some with verandas and stepladder entrances. Many were unoccupied during the winter months, while others were the permanent homes of young families or retired people. In the Jaywick Sands area, mainly in Beach Road (renamed Broadway in 1953), there were a number of two-storey houses and shops with flats above. Certain areas of Jaywick were unsewered and had no running water.

Three virtually separate areas together make up Jaywick; the triangle which is Jaywick Sands runs from north to south down Jaywick Lane into Golf Green Road, and then along the seafront up to Lion Point. In 1953, a concrete wall, maintained by the Essex River Board (ERB,) protected the Jaywick front as far as Lion Point.

West of Lion Point is Brooklands. Brooklands was built on privately reclaimed marshland. It was protected from water coming from the St Osyth marshes by a wall maintained by the ERB, and from the sea by a concrete wall built by the Jaywick Sands Freeholders Association (known locally as 'Adrian's Wall' after the Chairman, Adrian Wolfe).

The third area is Grasslands, a small corridor of bungalows hemmed in between the Essex River Board's wall at the back of Brooklands and a counter wall running inland from the sea. Unfortunately, the walls acted like the edges of saucers, trapping the water within when Brooklands and Grasslands flooded. It was later estimated that 250 chalets were occupied on the night of 31 January 1953.

The Harwich harbourmaster telephoned Divisional Headquarters at Clacton police station at 9.52 that night to warn of the predicted exceptionally high tide, and by midnight Clacton Police were dealing with the flooding in Harwich. There had been no report of problems from Jaywick, but the District Riverboard engineer at Clacton, aware of the vulnerability of Brooklands, told the police to warn Jaywick of the possibility of flooding, because of what was happening elsewhere.

Apart from the rain and gale-force wind blowing, Saturday had been a normal winter day for most Jaywick residents. At No. 278 Meadow Way, the home of 86-year-old James William Jew and his wife, Esther, there was a family gathering. Their son, James, and married daughter, Sarah Dempster, had joined them to celebrate Esther's 89th birthday on Sunday, 1 February. But in the night a great wave overwhelmed the house and all four were drowned. The police found their bodies on Tuesday. The birthday cake was untouched.

Life was about to change for all the people of Jaywick. Shortly after midnight, Mrs Allard, in her first-floor flat in Beach Road, the highest part of Jaywick, was called by a neighbour who said water was coming over the seafront. Mrs Allard, an officer of the Red Cross, immediately got up, put on all the lights and lit the fires. Two of Mrs Allard's near neighbours were brothers; Frank Allum, owner of Dot's Newsagents in Beach Road, and Denis, the sub-postmaster. The two, along with Mrs Allard's husband, went out to warn people to get upstairs if possible.

Young Miss Weatherburn of Meadow Way wrote of that fateful night:

' The Saturday before the flood was a dreadful day; terrific gales were blowing and it was raining nearly all day. I went to bed at about 11.45 but was soon awakened by my father. We saw that floodwater had rushed into our bungalow and was by then about 2 feet deep. After a terrific struggle we all managed to get up into the loft just as another rush of water came in, flooding up to the picture rail. It was a terrifying experience but I realised there was nothing more we could do to save ourselves.

We were all in our nightclothes with nothing on our feet, but it was when my father broke through the roof so that we could be seen that we felt really cold. During all this time I was aware of the frantic screams for help which were going on around us, but after a time everything was quiet. '

The local police had been alerted. Local bobby, PC Mitchell, had telephoned Clacton and reported that nine or ten people were trapped in Brooklands and that help was needed immediately. Experience of past floods meant the possibility of Brooklands flooding was topmost in everyone's thoughts. Soon after midnight, Frank and Denis Allum met Sergeant Saville and a local boatman, Jim Shepherd, in Beach Road. This small group were the key to the successful early rescue arrangements in Jaywick. It would be daylight before any large-scale rescue work commenced, and in the meantime Jaywick residents doggedly got on with the task of helping each other. The Allum brothers, Sergeant Saville and Jim Shepherd had just begun to manhandle a boat from the boat hut opposite the Morocco Café into the floodwater, when someone called for help. Two children and three women had been rescued from a flooded house on the seafront; one child had whooping cough and the grandmother, having been taken out of the window, had had a heart attack. Reluctant though they were to leave their families in Jaywick, Frank took the children to Clacton police station and Denis took the grandmother to Clacton Hospital, where he warned the matron that trouble was brewing in Jaywick. Mr Allen of HM Coastguards had, by that time, also begun to take people to Clacton Hospital in his car. He later put in a plea from Clacton fire station to Clacton Pier for all available boats to be sent to Jaywick.

The problems of rescue in Jaywick were immediately obvious to all. There was a fierce gale blowing and the weather was freezing cold, and, until dawn, very few boats were available. Two boats under repair and belonging to Syd Smith were put to use, with Syd taking one and boatman Jim Shepherd the other. PC Harry Mitchell found a rowing boat and set forth with the other local men to the rescue. They continued to work through the night and well into the next day, but it could never be enough; most people remained in their trapped and vulnerable homes till dawn at least.

The rescued and those who could make their own way arrived wet, cold and clad only in soaked nightclothes at Mrs Allard's flat. With a few helpers, Mrs Allard welcomed them with tea and warm clothes. She later wrote: 'Soon my home was full. Some of these poor things had to be carried up twelve steps to my flat. How everyone worked, including the police. There is no resident doctor in Jaywick, the lights failed at 1 a.m. and the telephones were no use. Undaunted, we worked on by candlelight.'

Hours later, when Mrs Allard's temporary unofficial rest centre was full, the Morocco Café, which stood on a small area of higher ground on the corner of Beach Road and Garden Road, was commandeered by the police for the purpose. Radiators were

The brave Allum brothers, who began rescue operations before dawn. (Courtesy of William Stevens)

put on, blankets borrowed and food and drinks organised for the survivors. Frantic and heartrending calls could be heard, from people trapped nearby, but safe in the café the 'Morocco team' were also trapped on their island.

At about 12.30 a.m. mountainous waves were seen rolling towards 'Adrian's Wall'. Water was pouring over it, running 1 foot deep down Tamarisk Way and Broome Way and flooding the marshes behind Brooklands. The tide turned soon after 1 a.m., but the gale-force wind whipped the water up, so that the level remained high, and both Brooklands and Grasslands were known to be badly flooded. However, 'Adrian's Wall' was still holding, the water was no longer rising and it was thought that the worst was over.

But disaster was fast approaching Jaywick from behind.

Shortly after 1 a.m., Inspector Barnicoat, with constables Joe Burgess and Don Harmer, arrived at Tamarisk Way in the wireless car (a police car with radio contact was then a new development). By chance, the Inspector turned to look inland at the marshes behind Brooklands. As he looked, the moonlit glassy surface was broken by 'what appeared to be a wide river of very turbulent water raging through the floodwater from inland'. In a flash he realised that there was danger coming from a new and quite unexpected direction. The Inspector saw an elderly couple, Mr and Mrs Roker, wading towards him, knee-deep in water. He rushed them into the car with his men and started the engine.

The Inspector's plan was to drive along Meadow Way and up Church Road (now St Christopher's Way), to higher ground at Beach Road, giving warning as they went. But the water came too fast for them. The car had only moved about 30 yards when water surged up around it. The engine stalled and Barnicoat saw 'a solid wall of water' bearing down on Meadow Way from the back, bringing masses of rubbish with it. The surge engulfed the car then fell away to about wheel level. The vehicle shuddered but did not overturn. In the few seconds before the water gathered itself and surged forward again, described later as the 'wall of death', they all escaped from the car, the constables carrying the old couple on their

Airmen going out to work on sea walls by searchlight. (Reproduced courtesy of Essex Record Office)

backs. Seconds later, the fierce current carried them helplessly away. Mr Roker lost his grip and fell into the churning water. Without hesitation Joe Burgess dived in and caught him as he lay head down, trapped under a hedge. With water lapping their necks, the car abandoned and all sense of direction lost, the flow of water swept them along and eventually brought them to the comparative safety of shallower water in Beach Road. Mr and Mrs Roker were taken to the rest centre at Mrs Allard's flat.

With the loss of the wireless car, there was no longer any communication between Jaywick and the Clacton Police headquarters. In order to get a message to the Clacton Police, 21-year-old PC Don Harmer, with incredible courage and determination, set out alone on a perilous journey. He struggled, chin-high in water, to the sea wall and crawled along it by moonlight in a gale, with

Devastated caravans near Jaywick's Martello Tower. (Courtesy of Essex Police Museum)

Firemen help survivors at the top of Jaywick Lane, furthest away
from the sea. (Courtesy of St Osyth Historical Society)

deep floodwater on one side, and on the other, the sea, ebbing but still high, turbulent
and washing over him. He reached the phone box, over a mile away, reported on the
situation in Jaywick, returned back again along the wall and turned up at about 3 a.m. at
the home of Mrs Allard. Mrs Allard told later how she 'saw a very young PC who sort of
sat down in my entrance hall, I thought he was just overcome by it all and I tried to cheer
him up and gave him a cup of tea. I found out later that this young man had crawled
along the sea wall to report to Clacton. He was all in, a brave boy indeed!' PC 196 Don
Harmer was later awarded the Queen's Commendation for Brave Conduct during the
1953 floods at Jaywick.

Sergeant Saville, outside the boat hut on Beach Road, also saw the surge approaching
and described it in the police report as 'a shining silver mass, gleaming brilliant in the
moonlight, sweeping up Cornflower Road and the other side roads, from Meadow Way,
towards Beach Road and the sea wall'. The sergeant and the boatman were on dry land
one minute, carrying the boat, but the next minute they launched the boat into the deep

water that met them in Cornflower Road. The two men pulled with all their strength on the oars to make headway against the wind and current, towards the pitiful cries they heard somewhere ahead of them among the rooftops.

The sudden surge had been caused by floodwater pouring through twenty-two breaches in the sea wall to the west, between Beacon Hill and Colne Point. This produced a vast mass of water, which then headed east across three and a half miles of St Osyth marshes to strike Jaywick at the back. As the surge advanced, the driving wind and the weight of the water joining the flow from thirty breaches along St Osyth beach increased its force and speed. So violent was its progress that it stripped the grass off the marshland and carried with it towards Jaywick a tangled mass of debris from smashed caravans.

Monty Dare of Jaywick, lodging in London, learned of the plight of his family when he spotted them in this photo on the front page of the *Daily Express* on 2 February. (Press Association)

Gathering speed as people slept, the torrent swept towards Meadow Way and Golf Green Road, the part of Jaywick farthest from the sea wall, where the ground is as much as 2 feet 6 inches below the high water mark of spring tides. No danger had been anticipated as coming from that direction, and no warning had been given or preparations made.

Seven people died in Golf Green Road that night and fifteen in Meadow Way.

When Frank Allum returned to Jaywick from Clacton he met the flood at the top of Golf Green Road. The night was full of cries and screams. He immediately helped a man struggling waist-deep in the water with a child on his shoulders. His brother returned at the same time, and together they went by car to the fire station to get high-ground clearance vehicles to help rescue people. At 2.55 a.m. they were standing outside the fire station shouting, 'They're drowning down in Jaywick'. They returned with the fire brigade to Jaywick Lane and joined the search and rescue operations there.

Throughout Brooklands, Grasslands and other parts of Jaywick, the sea had barged into the homes of sleeping residents, waking them in the early hours. Young Monty Dare's mother got up to go to the toilet and found the carpet coming up off the floor. She tried to run to wake everyone but it was like trying to run on a hammock; 'She ran like a drunken sailor, a crazy run with her legs going in all directions'. The bungalow, like many others, was standing on 2 foot brick piles, so with 3 feet of water in the bungalow, the overall depth of the floodwater was about 5 feet.

Among the rooftops in Meadow Way were Mr and Mrs Vivashi and their 8-year-old twins. They had been woken at about 2 a.m. by a terrific crash when their front door flew open and floodwater rushed in.

'We dashed out of bed and down the stairs. There was water gushing and swirling round our kitchen, with pots and pans clattering round. We went into the water in our night attire to rescue the children, and water was up to my armpits immediately. My husband disappeared into Marilyn's room, while I tried to get Martin. We had a sliding door which was jammed tight; I just could not move it. The water dragged me into another room, but I managed to pull myself back again. In Marilyn's room my husband was fighting his way in pitch darkness through the water when a large chest of drawers fell on him, trapping his foot. At last he struggled free and got Marilyn out. Then with a super-human effort he managed to force Martin's door open and we took the children upstairs. I shook from head to foot with shock. My husband looked out of the back window and saw that a large bungalow had lifted completely off its foundations, and he feared it might hit our home. There was water as far as you could see, and I thought we could never get out of it alive.'

Two strong firemen rescued the family by boat at about 9 a.m., when the water was level with the top of the front door. They were rowed up to the petrol station in Golf Green Road, where at last they reached dry land. An ambulance took them to the Osborne Hotel Clacton, where 'we were given a nice hot bath and a cup of tea'.

The mass of water from the St Osyth marshes further isolated the people on the Morocco Café 'island'. The Jaywick Lane rescue group were unaware of the safe 'island' near the sea wall, and no contact between the two groups was possible during the night. It was nearly daybreak when Frank and Denis made their way down Golf Green Road to Beach Road, and Frank found his family there safe and well. In the meantime, with Jaywick completely cut off from Clacton, the rescue force was complete. There would be no reinforcement until daylight.

At 11.35 a.m. on Sunday, 1 February, the police reported that water was still coming over the walls at Brooklands and Grasslands, and was 10 feet deep in places. Rescuers found people near collapse with shock and exposure, standing on windowsills and clinging to house eaves with their fingertips. Some, numbed by the cold, dropped into the water and drowned. Mr Handscombe, watching from Whyers Hall on higher ground in St Osyth, was horrified to see a whole Jaywick family, one by one, slip into the water and disappear. Those sheltering in roof spaces were almost as vulnerable; the lofts were cold and often no more than 18 inches in height. Victims lying flat on the rafters were rescued when hands were seen waving through holes knocked through roofs. Firemen used their axes to enlarge the holes, and survivors were pulled out and passed down to a rocking boat below.

More agile people were on the rooftops. Some, with water swirling around them, attached themselves to chimneypots while they waited and desperately hoped for rescue. Some bungalows seen floating in the strong current still had people clinging to the roofs twelve hours after the first flooding. When rescue came, boats were rowed directly onto rooftops and tied to chimneypots to enable victims to step straight in. Two pregnant women and a baby in a carrycot were carried out from rooftops in Brooklands. Jim Shepherd remembered one woman who had a parcel tucked in her blouse, which fell out when they beached. It contained £2,000.

Some bungalows were completely submerged. Residents who were unable to leave their homes immediately had little chance of escape.

The Clacton Lifeboat, *Sir Godfrey Baring*, was called to Jaywick on the afternoon of 1 February, and launched with a dinghy into very rough sea. The possibility of dropping rubber dinghies from the air to the marooned families had been discussed, but the strength of the wind was against it. The lifeboat coxswain manoeuvred the boat as near as possible to the sea wall; the crew manhandled the dinghy over it and rescued five men, one woman, two children, two dogs and a cat from the roof of a bungalow. The grateful passengers were given hot soup and blankets on board the boat, and taken to Clacton Pier.

Boatman and fisherman Dick Harman, along with other lifeboat men, returned to Jaywick from Clacton, bringing with them the Harry Welham rowing boats, which were stored at Pier Gap in winter. They were 14 feet long and could sit six to eight safely.

The conditions were grim and, even manned by strong and experienced boatmen, it was extremely difficult to row to the stranded families. The water was full of hidden obstacles and live with electricity; petrol was leaking from the garage, and people were lighting matches to show their positions, apparently unaware of the danger. But survivors were brought to dry land, wet, shocked and exhausted. Policemen's wives waded through the water to meet the boats with hot drinks and with blankets from their own beds.

At the height of the disaster, surrounded as it was by walls which separated it from the rest of Jaywick and from the marshland behind, Grassland resembled a saucer, brim-full of water, adrift in a turbulent sea. In 1953, the family of Harry Francis had recently moved to their bungalow in Grasslands after being bombed out at Elm Park. Thirteen-year-old Harry, shaken awake by his father, waded through deep water in his underpants to join his sister, perched on the kitchen table. He watched in fear as his mother slipped and was dragged under the water by her waterlogged nightdress, saving herself at last by grabbing the picture rail. Harry later told a *Clacton Gazette* reporter:

> Father smashed a hole in the ceiling and pulled the whole family up into the roof space. It was cold and pitch black. Dad then punched a hole in the end of the bungalow and called for help. At daylight we saw caravans and dead cows floating by. And then the next door bungalow! Then our bungalow floated off its base and started to move. By the afternoon there was still no sign of any rescuers and the house was still moving. It finally came to a halt wedged against a brick-built shed.

In all parts of Essex affected by the flood the Scouts could be relied upon to volunteer and to perform any necessary task. In Jaywick, 1st Clacton Scout Terry Hayward remembered rowing out alone in the middle of the night and bringing several people back to dry land. Cliff Marsh, of the same Troop, was remembered by many as the young man who rowed alongside the sea wall in the darkness, rescuing six people before his canvas canoe sank under him.

Miss Weatherburn peered out of the hole her father had knocked through the roof onto 'miles of water with just the tops of bungalows jutting out'. Rescuers could be seen but a very strong current was making their work extremely difficult. 'My father's two sisters, elderly ladies, lived in a bungalow opposite us and there was no sign of life there at all.' The sisters, 71-year-old Lavinia Lambert and Florence Weatherburn, aged 69, lived together at No. 95 Meadow Way. They were found dead in their beds on 2 February.

At one point, the police became very worried about the safety of PC Mitchell. He climbed onto a wall to rescue people, but it collapsed under him just as a great wave crashed over him. He surfaced and clambered onto the roof of a bungalow, pulled some

A flooded Street in Jaywick. (Press Association)

tiles off with his hands and dropped into a bedroom, where he found a man sound asleep. After seeing the man to rescue, PC Mitchell managed to get back to his colleagues hours later by climbing across the rooftops, safe but exhausted.

Temporary Jaywick residents Alex and Gilda Anthony had moved from Holland-on-Sea to a rented house in Sea Thistle Way while their house was being built. When woken in the night by floodwater, they made the decision to leave their home and find safety elsewhere. Gilda woke their two children, covered them with clothes and rushed them into the pram. At that moment the lights went out.

The family waded out of the house and, pushing the pram, headed towards the higher ground at Butlin's, near Clacton's Martello Tower. Water was creeping up around them as they battled on, and, nearby, people were struggling up to their armpits in water. They were halfway along the sea wall when the family were hit by a huge wave. The pram was snatched from their hands, overturned, and would have been carried out to sea had not a stranger dashed forward to help. Soaked, cold and traumatised, the family made it to the safety of Butlin's.

Harry Francis and his family were not rescued from Grasslands until midday on Monday the 2nd. Two men making a last check on the area heard their calls. They were taken by boat to the old sea wall at Midway, and from there, wet, hungry and exhausted, walked the two miles to the Morocco Café. There they were given very welcome blankets and hot drinks, before being rowed, like all the rescued from

Brooklands and Grasslands, across another saucer of deep and fast-flowing floodwater to dry land in Golf Green Road, where ambulances waited.

By midday on Sunday, boats and their crew had been brought to Jaywick from the fire stations at Clacton, Wivenhoe, Brightlingsea, Tiptree, Manningtree, Bradfield and Weeley. Co-operation between the police, the fire brigade and many civilian helpers resulted in a well-organised rescue operation. A reporter from the *Clacton Gazette* praised the way the rescuers toiled on without rest; 'All through the afternoon the pathetic convoy of tiny boats came in. Time and time again the tired, dirty, soaked policemen, firemen and civilians went back.'

Taken from the high point at the top of Golf Green Road, where police and ambulances waited. The sea lies straight ahead, beyond the houses in the distance. (Courtesy of Essex Police Museum)

The heroics of a taxi driver known as 'Dutch' was reported in the *Clacton Gazette*. His tale began at midnight on Saturday night, when he found and claimed a cockleshell dinghy to use in rescue work, and was joined by a youngster of about 18. Together they rowed up Meadow Way. To the left they heard someone hammering on a bungalow window; an old woman trapped and frightened. They turned towards the bungalow, but water began gushing into the dinghy, which was sinking. Frantically, they paddled to the safety of the bungalow and grabbed the guttering as the dinghy went down beneath them. They added their voices to the old lady's in crying for help, which came in the burly figure of Special Constable Batchelor. Back on dry land, the two rescued rescuers looked round for another boat.

Dutch acquired another boat and continued the search. He later told the tragic story of how he found one couple in the loft with their dog. He helped the man into his boat then put the dog on his lap. 'The woman, who was elderly, panicked. She slipped into the water and vanished in seconds. Nothing could be done. The old man just sat there holding the dog. He was a bundle of nerves and just could not realise what had happened.' In his many journeys past waterlogged houses, Dutch saw several floating bodies but, like all the rescuers, had to ignore them and concentrate on the living.

The County Welfare Officer at Jaywick reported that Dutch worked heroically day after day, despite knowing that his own parents were missing in the flood in Holland.

Miss Marie Miles was not one of the rescued. She lived with her sister Florence Miles at No. 3 Cornflower Road, directly in the path of the flood. In the late evening of that fateful day, Marie telephoned her friends, Mr and Mrs Reeves in Rosemary Way, and told them to get up into the loft immediately. Within minutes there was 8 feet of water in the friend's house, but the adults and two children were safe amongst the rafters.

The sisters prepared to leave their bungalow as soon as they became aware of the rising water. With desperate courage Florence carried her younger sister, who was unable to walk. Somehow they managed to get out through the window, but tragically, after getting so far, Marie was swept out of her sister's arms by the torrent crashing passed. Florence survived but Marie, aged 42, was drowned.

After the first exhausting day, the grim task of collecting bodies fell to the police and the lifeboat men. Every house was broken into and searched, as no records existed to show which were occupied. Dick Harman never forgot the harrowing task. 'Some bodies were frozen in grotesque shapes, in positions they had drowned in – perhaps after holding onto picture rails for hours or trying to get out.' The bodies could not be carried on a stretcher – a special van was brought in for the purpose.

When Roy Vaughan in Clacton heard of the disaster at Jaywick, he cycled there with his brother-in-law to check on his parents in Meadow Way. At the end of West Road 'the Martello Tower appeared to be floating on the sea, and at the bottom of the hill we could see Flaunty's Garage submerged'. The two men commandeered an old boat and set off along flooded Golf Green Road to search for the elderly couple, rowing with a plank of wood as an oar. They saw 'the Moorish architecture of the Morocco Café on its isolated island looking like a moated castle.' In the café they found Roy's parents. They had managed to get into the loft when the floodwater smashed into their home, and were rescued when the police boat was rowed straight through the door into the bungalow. Man and wife had to lie down in the boat in order to get back out of the door. Roy and his brother-in-law rowed the old couple in the overloaded boat back to where ambulances were waiting.

A week later, the family went back to the house and found the upturned table still afloat and on the table their dog, which they had assumed had drowned, still guarding the house.

Another dog, Rex, a border collie, saved the lives of his owners, Denis Abbot and his wife. At 12.20 a.m. the dog scratched their faces to wake them. When Denis jumped out of bed, he saw 7 feet of water flying past his window in Golf Green Road. The French window caved in and water reached the picture rail in seconds. The couple went on to the veranda and were rescued by the fire brigade in boats the next morning. The dog was trapped in the bedroom. Three days later, Denis's brother went back to the bungalow to look for the body of the dog, but he too was alive. A tearful reunion soon followed!

Faithful dogs abounded throughout Essex during the flood. A Jaywick ambulance driver was amazed to discover that a little black dog had followed the ambulance carrying his master the two miles to the hospital in Clacton.

The last person to be rescued from flooded Jaywick was 65-year-old Sister Louise Kemp. She too might have died if not for her tabby cat, Tiger. He pawed her as she lay sleeping and she awoke to see water swirling round her bed. When it rose higher she clambered on top of a wardrobe. Still the water rose. So, with a clothes hanger, she smashed her way through the ceiling, bundled Tiger through, and climbed up into the roof space. There, wrapped in a cotton nightdress and a sodden red blanket, she stayed, foodless, lightless and shivering all through that night and the following day. Rescuers searched throughout Sunday, but Louise was not known to have been missing and the bungalow had been marked as searched. Sister Kemp waved a distress signal through a small opening in the roof until, on Monday morning, she saw light filtering through the roof tiles. Later, in hospital, she told the Clacton police, 'I started whooping and cooing like the haunted, then I saw a hatchet knock through the tiles and the very welcome face of a policeman'. On Monday morning, after being trapped in her loft for thirty-one hours, Louise was taken from her home in Triumph Avenue. The police carried her to the safety of the Morocco Café, before taking her to Clacton Hospital. The three-man crew then returned to Triumph Avenue to rescue Tiger. Around his neck a boatman tied a label, 'Sister Kemp's cat'.

Travelling in his van at about 8 a.m. on Monday morning, Peter Wright and a colleague attempted to drive from Frinton to his work in Jaywick. At the junction of Golf Green Road, Crossways and Jaywick Lane, where the road dips, they met police cars and ambulances in shallow water, while below and in front of them, deep floodwater waited. The police were barring access to the flooded area, so they drove the van back to Butlin's in Clacton, walked back to Jaywick along the sea wall and collected a van that they kept there.

Peter, along with Jimmy, the local milkman, acquired a rowing dinghy and spent the day searching flooded bungalows which Jimmy knew to be occupied. The known survivors had already been rescued and people were carrying bodies along the sea wall from the worst affected areas to higher ground. Peter and Jimmy relieved the men of the grim and hazardous task of carrying the bodies through the water, by transporting them by boat and van to the checkpoint outside the Morocco Café.

In Meadow Way the two men found an elderly couple who had drowned. Peter later recalled what a gruesome task it was to get them to the dry spot where PC Mitchell, who knew their names, labelled them before sending them on to the ambulance at the petrol station. Years later, Peter said,

> The horror and tragedy of it meant nothing at the time. It sank in later. I remember particularly coming along to the corner of Beach Road and Lavender Way. Here we found four bodies the boatmen had loosely attached to a telegraph pole to stop them from floating away. At Singer Avenue in Grasslands, a gentleman brought out a woman, and two others were carrying a young boy. I'd never seen drowned people before. I could not take it in, but later the dreadful sadness of it sank in and I've never forgotten the sight of that poor child.

The tragic victims of Singer Avenue were Lillian Darvill, who was pregnant, and her 11-year-old son, Michael. Lillian's brother had called into the rest centre every day, searching for his sister and nephew. He learned of their fate when lists of fatalities were published three days later.

At about midday, Peter and Jimmy had another heartrending experience:

> We were in Cornflower Road, outside a little bungalow, no. 27. The front garden was nothing but brambles so we decided that no one lived there. But at that moment a young man appeared beside us and attempted to get into the house, insisting that his parents were inside. The police at first tried to dissuade him, but he disregarded them and, wading into the water, began to push back the brambles shouting, 'My mother and father are in there', and they were.

Percy Willson was the young man, and he later told how he entered the bungalow with a police officer and found the bodies of both his parents, Lucy and Samuel Willson, in the floodwater in the kitchen. Percy then took on the harrowing task of helping the police officer to carry his dead parents out of their home and travelling with them to the mortuary.

When the worst was over, calling for survivors. (Courtesy of Jaywick Local History Society)

Days went by as police, firemen and civilian volunteers worked tirelessly with little or no sleep. When Inspector Barnicoat returned from a rescue mission, the *Clacton Gazette* reported, 'His eyes were red with strain, his face ashen as he was helped from the boat. He was told to go home and rest, but refused and went off again'.

The Clacton hotels reacted without hesitation in offering accommodation to the homeless. One hundred and twenty people took up the offer of free rooms, baths and meals. They were later rehoused in caravans at the Valley Farm camping site. And at the Morocco Café, after the rescued had been fed and cared for by Mrs Allard and her band of helpers, the police and rescue workers were given hot meals for a week.

Many elderly persons coped well with the loss of their homes and almost all their possessions, but grieved over their lost spectacles and false teeth. One old man had even watched helplessly as his wooden leg floated out of the window. His leg was recovered later and dried out in an airing cupboard in Oulton Hall Hotel, where he was housed.

6

ST OSYTH AND POINT CLEAR

The parish of St Osyth is extensive, covering the area from the creek of the Colne, opposite Brightlingsea, to Clacton-on-Sea. The centre of the village, with its medieval priory, is a designated conservation area. To the west of the village centre is Point Clear and Point Clear Bay.

On the night of 31 January 1953, the Causeway at Mill Dam was under water by 11.40 p.m. The St Osyth constable phoned the sergeant in Clacton and then warned the houseboat residents to vacate their boats. He spent the rest of the night stopping people from driving into the water. One group

Seawick Sands, St Osyth. Caravanners spent the night on the double-decker bus and climbed to safety from the upper windows the day after the flood. (Courtesy of St Osyth Historical Society)

A double-decker bus gets caught in the flood in Marsh Road, Manningtree.(Courtesy of Manningtree Museum)

returning from a late dance did just that and were lucky to survive. By high tide at 1 a.m., the Causeway was under 5 feet of water and the great surge had lifted the houseboats from their moorings and flung them like toys onto the Causeway.

Below the village, in the caravan park at Seawick Sands, weekenders were out in the open on the beach, watching the thunderous seas when the wall gave way. They ran for shelter to a double-decker bus, which was parked on the site awaiting renovation, and there, as the water rose and the night grew colder, they were marooned for the night. No one knew of their plight until Sunday morning, when the village of St Osyth awoke. Mr Handscombe of Whyers Hall looked out at the marshes and the caravan site below his house and telephoned the Clacton Police to report that the caravans were under water to their roofs. Terry O'Dell was woken at his home in Beach Road by a young man who informed him, 'Mr O'Dell, your camp is underwater.' Mr O'Dell borrowed a dinghy and oars in order to row out to the caravan site, as his sister and her husband, along with several other residents who were staying at the site, would be in peril.

At about the same time, St Osyth resident Syd Bruce cycled towards the beach and met the water's edge below Whyers Hall (now the Good Life Inn). The marshes were under water, and about a hundred caravans were wrecked and lying about. The police were kept informed by Mr Handscombe, who reported mid-morning that the people were safe on the top deck of the bus, but that the tide was coming in again and the wind was rocking the vehicle. But St Osyth was cut off from Clacton and Jaywick. No one could get through overland and no Jaywick boats were available.

The St Osyth rescuers wasted no time. Mr Handscombe sent a lorry carrying a large boat to the water's edge. Herbert Lewis, Ben Richardson, Syd Bruce, Foster Jacobs and John Scolding were the crew, and the five rowed out towards the stranded bus.

Terry O'Dell and his helper in their dinghy reached the bus with the only supplies he could grab before setting off: a carton of cigarettes and half a bottle of brandy.

Syd Bruce wrote later, 'We found people including an elderly lady on the top deck. Their weight made the bus top heavy and the wind and waves appeared about to topple the bus. We knocked out a window in the top deck. I stood up in the boat and they crawled out over my back, not an easy job with the wind and waves buffeting the boat against the bus.' Several trips were made by the rescue boats and eventually all reached dry land and safety.

Survivors from the bus voiced their concerns about a young man, Reg Arthur, and his mother, who had been heard calling in the night but of whom nothing had been heard since. Knowing roughly where they lived, Syd and the crew set off to look for the couple, calling as they went. At last, faint calls echoed back and the bungalow was found. Mother and son could be seen huddled on the ceiling joists with the water just 12 inches below.

Reg Arthur told his story in the *St Osyth News* on Saturday, 31 January 1953:

' The loft was windowless with no means of escape, but I managed to batter a hole through one of the metal lath and plaster gable ends as an escape route and to see what was happening.

Almost as soon as this was done, we were shocked to see a small haystack floating by in the brilliant moonlight. More worrying still was when a complete bungalow, built similarly to ours, slowly drifted away after being lifted off its foundations.

It was a long night. When daylight came, it was obvious the water was far too deep for escape and we began to worry about the next high tide due soon after midday. Not realising the scale of the event, we reassured ourselves that help would soon be officially organised and on its way to us. Occasionally I called out in the hope of being heard.

It was almost time for the next tide when we heard voices and called out in response. Soon a sturdy boat and the familiar faces of Foster Jacobs and Syd Bruce among the crew came into view. Our legs were cold and numb but we were carefully helped down from our escape hole. '

The Arthurs' bungalow. Note the ruined furniture in the garden. Reg and his mother spent twelve hours on the rafters and climbed out through the gable ends. (Courtesy of St Osyth Historical Society)

Syd Bruce continues the story: 'We set off for home and the trouble began. The heavily laden boat was hard to row against the wind. Our oars were constantly hitting the barbed wire fencing of the grazing marsh and other hidden objects. We started to drift towards the breached sea wall and the open sea beyond, and were out in the middle of the marsh almost to Jaywick when Foster, who only had one hand and a hook, suggested that he should act as a Cox, using his oar as a rudder. We finally landed in the field next to the road'.

Reg and his mother were taken to Whyers Hall, where 'welcome food and dry clothing were arranged for us, and we were allowed to stay in warmth and comfort for several days while we recovered and planned for the future'.

Meanwhile, there was concern about the occupants of Marsh Cottage. The cottage was only a quarter of a mile from safety, but nothing had been heard of the elderly couple who lived there since the disaster occurred. Syd Bruce and crew made a brave attempt to rescue them, with no roads or familiar signs visible to guide them; but, beaten by the gale-force wind which almost capsized them, the men reluctantly returned to land.

Mr and Mrs Higgins, the owners of Marsh Cottage, later told their friend Charles Langlands that they had been stranded upstairs in bed, with the sea covering the floor of their bedroom and no heat, no food and no drinking water, from Saturday night until late Sunday afternoon. They had seen boats go past but were unable to attract their attention and had realised they would probably die of cold.

A second rescue attempt was made by Foster Jacobs, John Scolding, John White and Tony Cole, but the strength of the wind made it impossible to reach the cottage in a rowing boat, so the Navy were called in. With the help of local volunteer, Dr Norris, the stranded couple were finally rescued by sailors in a motorboat at about 3 p.m. on Sunday.

The story of the McGregor family is the stuff of nightmares. Sometime before midnight on that fateful night, teenage son Malcolm (Mac) looked out of the window of their bungalow in Leewick and saw, in the bright moonlight, that seawater had surrounded their home. Within minutes the family – parents, younger son Ian and young daughter Janet

Malcolm McGregor, who alerted his family and rowed them to safety. (Courtesy Malcolm McGregor)

– were rushed out of the door. Mr McGregor then returned to the house for an eiderdown for Janet, ill with pneumonia, but indoors the rising water forced the lino up, jamming it against the closed door and trapping him inside. Within those few minutes the water had risen to 5 feet and Mac had to move quickly to hack the door open with an axe. The family set out in their rowing boat for higher ground across the marshes, with Janet wrapped in her eiderdown, and her pony, tied to the stern, swimming behind.

In the howling wind, their boat overloaded and shipping water, almost overwhelmed and hampered by submerged fences, they battled their way forward. The nightmare worsened when Ian fell overboard and his clothes became entangled in wire. As they struggled frantically to release him, a great wave broke the sea wall and the sea level increased immediately from 5 to 10 feet. Paradoxically, the surge saved them by lifting them clear of the barbed wire

Janet McGregor holding the pony which swam behind the boat. (Courtesy of Malcolm McGregor)

and hurling them inland where they met, broadside on, the water bursting through the breaches in the wall between Leewick and Beacon Hill. The man and boys were back in the boat and rowing, but before long two of their three pairs of oars were blasted out of their hands when the blades were lifted out of the water. Their neighbour, Phyllis Hendy, wrote in her book *The Treacherous Tide*, 'Only the strength of the three men used to the sea brought them out alive. After two hours battling with the elements they brought the boat to dry land in a field of Brussels sprouts at Leewick Farm and walked to the farmhouse, the pony following them'. Their bungalow was thrown 60 yards across the marsh.

Tragically, two people, Mr and Mrs Crosswell, lost their lives in St Osyth due to the flood that night. Their son, Ronald, told the Clacton Police their tragic story:

‘ My father, William John Crosswell, aged 58, and my mother Lilian Crosswell, aged 58, were the proprietors of Crosssswell's Stores at Point Clear Bay and resided in the living quarters at the rear of the grocery shop. I am their only son. About 12.30 a.m. on Sunday, 1 February 1953 I saw that the tide, which was incoming, was very high in Point Clear Bay, and instead of following its normal channel it was sweeping diagonally across the sands to the sea wall, which is something I had never seen before in the seven years I have spent there. ’

Ronald called to his wife, 'Come and look at this. You will never see anything like this again'. The view was spectacular but, with the gale-force wind behind it, Ronald recognised the danger to his parents in their shop, situated low behind the sea wall. He phoned the shop and his surprised father got out of bed to answer:

'Hello, what do you want?' I told him the tide was very high and beginning to lap the top. He put the phone down and I heard him say to my mother, 'It's flooded outside'. I heard her reply in an agitated manner and he replied to me, 'All right' and replaced the receiver. I went outside to go down the slope to their house, a mere 300 yards away, and soon found myself up to my thighs in water. Finding I couldn't get through I went back to my place and phoned again. My father said, 'The shop floor's awash and I'm putting the goods up higher'. I told him to get some dry clothes and a towel and go to Steven's bungalow next door to the shop. He said, 'It's knee-deep now'.

Ronald's mother then came to the telephone, very alarmed. When asked where his father was, she replied, 'Walking up and down'. Ronald continued,

I was upset so I walked along the sea wall until I was close to their residence, but I could see I would not be able to reach them, so I went back to my house and phoned again. My father answered and he said, "The windows are coming in". Then my mother spoke. I told her I had tried to get to them. She sobbed, "Save yourself, I'm drowning". Then the phone went dead. With the help of Mr Glanfield and others, and after visiting several marooned persons, we finally arrived at my parents' shop in this boat. I could get no reply to shouts, the water being up to the eaves of the shop, so I broke a window of the sitting room with my oar and saw by the light of the torch my mother's face as she was floating in the water.

In all flooded areas, rescue of the living took precedence over recovery of bodies. The bodies of Mr and Mrs Crosswell were recovered two days later. They are buried in the local cemetery – the inscription on the gravestone reads:

They were lovely and pleasant in their life
And in their death, they were not divided.

With telephone and electricity cables down since 1 a.m. on Sunday, no contact could be made with Clacton until the River Board engineer, Mr Rolls, managed to cross the causeway on the ebbing tide at 4.45 a.m. From a phone box in the St Osyth village he reported on the situation. But the Clacton police were desperately searching for boats to rescue people trapped in Jaywick and could offer no help.

A rare picture of Crosswell Stores at Point Clear surrounded by floodwater:
no one survived. (Courtesy of St Osyth Historical Society)

Like their neighbours at Jaywick, the folk of Point Clear and St Osyth collected boats and looked after their own. Miles Simeon realised as early as 6 a.m. that flooding had occurred and went immediately to the Point with his small boat and rescue crew of five – himself, Bill Lilley, Dennis Barnes, John Austin and another man. Eventually, a group of Salvation Army bandsmen turned up to join the search, and a detective constable arrived to assist the local bobby. On the marshes the floodwater lay 8-12 feet deep and flowed inland for about a mile.

The licensee of the Coronation Club, a single-storey building, climbed onto the roof and spent a miserable and terrifying night alone, while two men in the Ferry Boat Inn were able to escape upstairs, probably carrying a few bottles! They were the last to be rescued.

One elderly man slept soundly through the raging storm. In his exposed house, built on piles on the saltings outside the sea wall and near the boat ferry to Brightlingsea, he awoke the next morning to an altered world.

7

BRIGHTLINGSEA

At Brightlingsea, in the Colne estuary, the Surveyor to the Urban District Council noticed the exceptionally high water at 11.30 p.m. and went to open the flood valves. But on reaching the Western Promenade Pleasure Grounds at midnight it was already too late – the grounds were flooded. Along with the police, he began to warn people living in the lower part of the town, and by 12.30, water flowing from the flat land to the north of the town had flooded the roads nearest the sea wall. Then, at 1 a.m., a second rush of water surged over the same marshes, drowning fifty sheep and marooning the sewage works attendant and his family in the upper floor of their house. The Brightlingsea branch line was swamped and not ready for use again until December 1953.

The Automobile Association (AA) patrol men were a familiar sight in Essex and they proved their worth during the emergency. The contribution of AA man R.H. Cawthorne, of Brightlingsea, was reported in the *Essex Chronicle* on 13 February 1953.

On Sunday, 1 February he remembered that two old ladies lived in almshouses in Lower Park Road. He reached their house, even though the water was chest high and floating sheep barred his way. Realising the water was too high and the tide too strong to carry people out, Mr Cawthorne told the newspaper:

‘ I first ascertained that they were alive and told them to hang on to the top window ledge while I returned for a boat. I next contacted the local policeman and two helpers and we rescued one lady after sinking one boat. The second lady wouldn’t come into the boat, so I went home for a flask of tea for her and passed it through the window. Some two hours later I got four chaps to push a four-wheeled horse cart to the garden fence and I balanced on the window ledge, supporting a plank to the cart while the old lady crawled out. I then carried on down Lower Park Road, checking at each house to see if the people were alright upstairs till the tide went down. ’

Sixty houses were flooded, three families were made temporally homeless and from one of these, with the family marooned upstairs, a boy swam ashore for assistance. But unlike some Essex areas, floodwater flowed away with the ebb tide.

Santiago Cottages,
Lower Park Road,
Brightlingsea. (Courtesy of
Brightlingsea Museum)

Destroyed beach huts at
Brightlingsea. (Courtesy of
Brightlingsea Museum)

By 7 a.m. on Sunday, the Clacton Police were aware of the disastrous situation in Jaywick and the assistant divisional officer was sent to Brightlingsea for boats. He arrived at 8 a.m. and sought out a retired sea captain, whom he knew to be a member of the county fire brigade committee. The captain, expecting a high tide after the gale, had had his sea boots and oilskins handy all night in case of a call out. 'We had our own troubles in Brightlingsea', he recalled, 'but we heard that about seven hundred people resident in Jaywick that night had no chance of getting out, owing to the fast rising tide.'

With the co-operation of the Brightlingsea harbourmaster, the hardmaster, lorry owners and the bosun of James's shipyard, boats were commandeered, oars and rowlocks borrowed and the lot loaded up and sent off to Jaywick with Brightlingsea seafaring men to crew them. Town ambulance personnel and members of the British Red Cross joined the men on the journey and helped care for survivors. Ten boats had arrived at Jaywick by 10.45 a.m. and the work of rescue began to make more progress.

8

WIVENHOE

Wivenhoe is situated on the east bank of the River Colne, above Brightlingsea. There is no sea wall on the quay and at high tide water often laps over onto the road. Facing the quay are the jumbled and picturesque streets of the old town, and behind these the main residential area rises up the hill away from the river.

An isolated house on Canvey Island. This photograph is an icon of the 1953 flood in Essex. (Reuter's image, reproduced courtesy of Essex Record Office)

On the night of the flood, older seafaring residents living on the quayside became concerned about the height of the tide and, expecting trouble, rolled up their mats and carpets in good time. Most households in the lower part of town had a tried and tested system for dealing with floods, which came into play that night when a tremendous volume of water came over the quay very quickly and burst into their houses. Fortunately, the water flowed away from the town on the ebb tide.

The occupants of Toll Gate House were not so fortunate. Their isolated home stood at the end of a private road adjoining the marshes. When floodwater surged across the marshes to their cottage, three people were marooned upstairs, with water up to the kitchen ceiling. Outbuildings were washed away and the house was in danger of collapse. But the elderly couple, unperturbed, refused to leave until the press photographer arrived to take a snap of them as they climbed out of the bedroom window. Firemen from Colchester rescued them by boat at noon on Sunday.

Forty-three houses were flooded in Wivenhoe, but of these only Toll Gate House was left uninhabitable. The Chairman and members of the Wivenhoe Urban District Council, with the surveyor and a police constable, went from house to house in the affected area, checking the damage and making sure no one was trapped. Each flooded household received a gift of 5cwt of coal from the council.

At 5.40 a.m. on Sunday, Wivenhoe's part-time firemen were called to Jaywick by a remote-controlled siren operated from Colchester. One of the part-time firemen was an electric welder and riveter from the shipyards at Wivenhoe. After toiling on the oars from dawn till dusk on Sunday, he gripped his large white mug of tea for warmth, and his work-hardened hands, rubbed raw, painted the mug red with blood.

In Wivenhoe, as in Brightlingsea, the railway lines were flooded and no trains ran to or from Colchester. The Eastern National Bus Company provided a temporary bus service and trains were again running by 3 February.

9

MERSEA ISLAND

Mersea Island lies between the estuaries of the Colne and Blackwater rivers. It is the most easterly inhabited island in the British Isles and is approximately eight miles from Colchester. The island is separated into West and East Mersea; West being the area with the larger population, and East the more rural.

At times of normal high tides, the only road which connects Mersea to the mainland, The Strood, is covered with water. On the night of the flood, the water surrounding the island, in the wide mouth of the River Blackwater and in the Colne estuary, resembled heavy seas. At 10.30 p.m. the Strood was already under water with two hours to go

STRUGGLING ACROSS THE STROOD!

← MERSEA

The Strood on a normal high tide. (Author's collection)

A typical sea wall breach. (Courtesy of Essex Police Museum)

before high tide. By 1.30 a.m. the water was 6 or 7 feet deep, and the Strood could not be crossed on foot or by vehicles until 3.30 a.m. on Monday. The B1025 Colchester to Mersea road was under water to the Peldon Rose public house, almost a mile away.

West Mersea rises fairly steeply from the sea. Boatyards, houseboats, huts, yachts and houses near the beach were potentially vulnerable, but all escaped serious flooding that night. However, gale-force winds and crashing waves wrecked boats at the sea wall and ripped them from their moorings. Mersea fishermen enjoyed recounting how one yacht, the *Ruddy Sheldrake*, broke from her moorings and 'ran like a loose horse, 100 miles across the North Sea to Holland'. A fishing smack and a skiff blew across the Blackwater to Bradwell and rowing boats disappeared never to be seen again.

The Clacton lifeboat *Sir Godfrey Baring* was called to Mersea Island on 1 February, to assist twenty people living on houseboats, which the wind and storm had lifted from their moorings and dropped randomly onto the saltings. The badly shaken owners were evacuated and went to stay with friends and relatives.

Along the River Blackwater, between Mersea Strood and Maldon, the violent sea crashed through the protecting walls in countless places. The Essex River Board employed men to walk the sea walls of Essex; one man was responsible for walking a fixed length of wall regularly once a month, in order to report on its condition. Instructions typed in the wall walkers' notebooks stated: The wall should be walked immediately after a storm or exceptional tide and any serious trouble requiring immediate attention should be notified by telephone as soon as possible.

The wall walkers of the Brightlingsea to Maldon sections were told on the afternoon of 31 January to walk their walls at daylight on Sunday, because the day's stormy weather might have caused damage. They began their work as usual at first light, under appalling conditions.

At approach points, what looked like a vast calm lake hid roads and deep marshland drainage ditches. Familiar landmarks such as gates and fences were now submerged obstacles and traps. The wall walkers of Essex, unsung heroes, made their way – usually alone – along miles of soaked and crumbling bank, with the greasy mud sucking at their feet at every step. In some parts, the landward side of the wall had been scoured out, leaving a hollow shell on top, too fragile for a man's weight; in others, the top of the wall had been washed off, and in some, hundreds of yards of wall had been blasted into the surrounding marshland, leaving nothing above salting levels. One wall walker between Mersea Strood and Saltcott became stranded on the one section of wall still standing as the tide came in and had to be rescued by boat. Another, after covering six miles, came to a wide impassable breach and had to walk the whole distance back. They gave the usual brief and precise details in their notebooks, giving no hint of risks taken or dangers encountered.

10

TOLLESBURY

The village of Tollesbury lies on the mouth of the River Blackwater, facing Mersea to the north and Bradwell to the south. The village's main road slopes down to marshlands and saltings, where there are boatbuilding yards and a small, safe and peaceful yacht harbour.

Mrs Symonds and her family saw a different view of the harbour on the night of the flood on their 80-foot yacht, *Herga*:

> In the moonlight it was an uncanny sight to see boats large and small breaking adrift. All the sea walls were under and we could see brilliant green electrical flashes as the houseboats in Mersea broke adrift and the power cables parted. Next morning was a scene of complete chaos. We were on the top saltings at a precarious angle and all around were other boats lying on their sides. The sea wall was a mass of wreckage and some boats were over in the marsh.

Walter 'Navvy' Mussett, an experienced stowboat fisherman, and his crew came very close to losing their lives to the treacherous seas off Tollesbury that evening. He never forgot his dramatic battle against the storm that night:

> Our smack dragged her anchor, and drifted onto Cob Marsh Island at about noon on that Saturday and we were unable to get to her until the tide flowed again at about 11 p.m. After attending a dinner and dance I changed into my sea clothes and went down to the hard to our foot boat (a 14-foot dinghy) with my crew of two, Mr Chatterson and 70-year-old 'Happy' Barbrook. We endeavoured to reach our smack but at Whale Point, which was about halfway, a terrific squall of wind and sleet blew up from the north-west which hampered us from rowing.

Navvy had no way of knowing that a tidal wave was approaching. He was at sea in a rowing boat at the worst possible time.

> The sea walls were gradually disappearing. We were unable to pull against the wind any longer, so we threw our anchor over with 15 fathoms of rope, but that was

The tide washed over the marshland like a waterfall.

useless, so we took to the oars again, pulling until we were exhausted. We were being carried towards the sea wall, with the tide washing over like a waterfall into the marshland, which is about 20 feet below. We now arrived at a critical moment; I shouted to my crew to make my voice heard above the noise from the wind and tide, 'jump onto the wall and hold the head of the boat pointing to sea'. But before they could do so a wave hit them and they were carried with the tide down the sea wall. I was standing waist-deep in water holding onto the boat, trying to swing her round when the crew managed to get back in. Then I jumped in. The tide was now pushing past us like a torrent, carrying us across the marshland. We bailed out the boat with our caps as she was half filled with water. We were about halfway across when we manoeuvred the boat to the lower part of the field adjoining the marshland and belonging to Woodrolfe Farm.

We were frozen stiff and our teeth were chattering like cups and saucers when we eventually arrived home at about 4.30 a.m. After a rub down and a change of clothes, a cup of tea and a double whiskey, I went to bed for an hour. Unable to sleep, I rose, dressed and went to my son's house and together we went down, borrowed a foot boat and rowed to where my smack was, which was as close to the sea wall as it could be. That gave us the job of digging her out, which took us three weeks to do.

'

11

HEYBRIDGE AND MALDON

That night, the North Sea rushed unheeded down the River Blackwater, overtopping and breaching the sea wall in countless places. In the early hours of that morning, Mr and Mrs White were driving home along the Goldhanger Road from a party and, knowing the tide was likely to be high, drove into Basin Road to check whether the water was over the wall. There they met a member of the Stebbins family ('all sailing men'), who was of the opinion that the tide was receding. But when they reached the little bridge, a huge quantity of water stopped them in their tracks and flooded the car. The couple put the car seats on the roof and, clambering up, spent the rest of the night in their party clothes, perched on top.

John Wakelin of Millbeach later described what had happened. Between Goldhanger and Heybridge, a breach just east of Osea Road had completely washed out the Fort sluice near Decoy Point, lifted 30 yards of sea wall into the Heybridge countryside and surged down Goldhanger Road like a river.

However, as the Whites drove into the road, only the cattle on Heybridge meadows had seen that the sluice had blown. The breach lessened the pressure on the sea walls as far as Maldon, hence why the 'Basiner' believed that the tide had ebbed. The surge then swept over the fields unchecked and hit them from behind.

The village of Heybridge Basin, known locally at the time as 'Cannibal Island', was among the very few places to benefit from the flood. The 'Cannibals' (as the locals were known) found an unexpected harvest of fish in the canal lock when the tide went down, which they boxed and sent to Billingsgate post haste.

Nearby at Mill Beach camping ground, on the Goldhanger Road, the caretaker and his wife were woken by the rocking movement of their caravan at about 1.30 a.m. Outside, water was waist deep, caravans were toppled and floating, and one had been lifted and dropped onto the sea wall.

Police officers Suttling and Bailey were on duty that night. Tony Suttling later told how he walked, waded and swam his beat that night, and at the Mill Beach camping ground found dazed and freezing campers trying to help others trapped in their overturned and floating caravans.

Caravans at Mill Beach Camp Site, Heybridge. (Courtesy of Matthew Kingston)

At the Osea Camp Site, adjacent to Mill Beach, the steward awoke on hearing a dustbin hitting the side of his bungalow. He escaped with his family and woke the site owner and farmer, Mr Speakman of Vaulty Manor. Mr Speakman's immediate concern was for his pedigree Friesian heifers, which slept in the lee of the sea wall, near the old Decoy marsh, but he found the animals had made their way to safety on higher ground.

The breach at Decoy Point proved impossible to fill with sandbags. Local people – farm labourers mostly – worked to repair it by bulldozing one of the inland containing walls to form a great horseshoe to close the breach.

The town of Maldon, on its hill and slightly further along the Blackwater, was not seriously affected by the flood, but at Maldon Hythe, rival fisher families, the Pitts and Wrights, watched the rising tide and argued about possible consequences. One family determined to stay on board and mind their boats, the others, more relaxed, laughed and went home. It was soon the turn of the cautious family to laugh and jeer as they secured their own craft against the mounting swell, but when the boats rocked and crashed against the harbour walls, rivalry was soon forgotten as those on board made their rivals' boats secure.

At the bottom of Maldon's hill there was 2 feet of water in houses on the Causeway, and in Heybridge, The Square and Hall Road were similarly flooded. But, except in the

The town of Maldon from the Hythe. (Patricia Rennoldson Smith)

flooded cellars of pubs such as at the Queen's Head in The Street, water flowed straight out on the ebb tide.

In 1953, before the Blackwater was dammed, a creek, wide and deep, ran behind Hall Road, Heybridge, ending in the Square. Eileen Cannom, aged 13 at the time, was first up that morning in the family home in Spring Lane, off Hall Road, and was horrified to find their dog on the kitchen table with floodwater up to his belly. Their sturdily brick-built home suffered irreparable damage as floodwater entered the house on every high tide after that day. All houses by the creek were flooded, some up to 4 feet. All were eventually condemned and demolished.

People who lived near the coast of Essex were used to floods, but as one old Heybridge lady remarked to a member of the Maldon WVS who gave her a parcel, 'I bin flooded ever so many times but I *never* had a parcel before'.

12

BRADWELL

The entire Dengie peninsula presents an exposed front to the sea, and Bradwell, situated on the mouth of the Blackwater, occupies the northernmost spot. The foundations of a third-century Roman fort are concealed near the beach, and the seventh-century Church of St Peter-on-the-Wall stands proudly aloof there, above the marshes. On the night of the flood, the sea wall, which encircles the peninsula from Bradwell Quay to St Peter's chapel, took a terrific pounding; the sea stormed through at least twenty-four breaches, some as much as 200 yards wide, lowering the wall down to just 2 foot above the saltings in places.

The part of Bradwell village that sits at the waterside rises gently away from the waterfront and is rarely flooded, though there is nothing to stop the tide flowing over the quay at high water. On Saturday, 31 January everything appeared normal to the Bradwell constable, PC Booth, who stood keeping an eye on things from the corner by the Waterside post office. Booth knew nothing of the high tide warning, but he had noticed in the afternoon that the ebb tide had not gone far out and that the wind seemed to be holding up the water. The nearby Green Man pub had a licence extension until 11.30 that night and after the guests had left, the constable suddenly noticed that the quay at the bottom of the road had disappeared under water, and that water was gradually advancing up the slope towards him in a 'strange, calm almost purposeful way'. From the quay the water spilled round sideways behind the sea wall, which was still visible, towards the coastguard cottages. It was just after 11.30 p.m.

As the constable watched, the wind suddenly strengthened and seemed to heave the water forward without ruffling it, but lifting it in a mass. With the water rushing up the street towards him, Booth realised that the nearest bungalow to the sea wall was occupied and in great danger. By chance, a boat floated up the street from the direction of the quay. He waded towards it, and pushed it before him, down to the bungalow. There he found and rescued a man, a woman and three cats marooned on the table, with the water washing in underneath them. He pushed the boat back up to the Green Man, where the tide had halted, and the landlord and his wife took man, woman and cats in for the night, provided hot drinks and hot baths all round, and a pair of dry trousers for the policeman. PC Booth then went home to bed.

After a little more than an hour in bed, PC Booth was called by the Maldon police regarding a houseboat adrift at Mersea with people aboard. He decided to get to the sea wall beyond Marsh House Farm to see whether he could spot the houseboat, a journey which involved cycling from Bradwell to Tillingham, then down the lane to Leggatts and on to Marsh House. At Marsh House he met the water and realised for the first time that something serious was happening. He waded knee-deep to rouse the farm foreman, Leonard Raven. Raven was the only person who could follow the hidden paths through the water to the sea wall, and from that morning every horse or cart taken to the sea wall was led by him. Booth returned to Leggatts at about 4 a.m. and noted that from where he stood, water could be seen covering land both north and south of the Dengie Marshes.

The constable then cycled back though Bradwell towards Sandbeach Farm to warn the occupants, and at Hockley Farm he met farmer Mr Serrell-Watts. Floodwater prevented them from continuing their journey but as they searched around for a boat, a young farmer at Hockley Farm, who was new to the district, told them he had been near Sandbeach Farm, duck shooting by moonlight, when the water came over the wall. He had left his car there and waded home, telling nobody of the flood; however, he confirmed that Sandbeach House, on its slight hump, was not flooded.

Mr Serrell-Watts kept an account of the night and wrote of how he chanced to meet PC Booth:

❝ I was awakened at 4.45am by a voice calling, which I thought was my cowman. I got
up and shouted out of the window, 'What the hell do you want?' I then realised it was
my foreman, who told me that the sea wall at Weymarks was down.

I set out with my foreman to walk towards Weymarks but found that there was
3 feet of water over the road, so we made our way to Hockley Farm. Having passed the
farmhouse we saw a light approaching and reasoned that there was no water on the

Marsh House
Farm, Tillingham,
on the Dengie
peninsula.
(Courtesy of
Kevin Bruce)

road but soon discovered it was our policeman, Mr Booth, pushing his bike through the water. He had been attempting to get to Sandbeach Farm but the depth of water had beaten him in spite of his valiant effort, particularly as he was new to the district and had no real knowledge of where the roads and ditches lay. Booth then went home and we went back to Weymarks to wait for daylight, when we could look for the seventy cattle which were on the Hockley Marsh. We got a saddle horse and cart with some hay and a horseman ready and we got to Hockley Marsh at about half past 7, when it had begun to get light. The cattle had been in the water and were very cold and wet but had congregated on a piece of grass on high land, surrounded by a 3-4 foot deep moat, which they would have to cross to safety. Eventually, we persuaded the horse with the cart and the hay, with some difficulty, to go through this deep water and the cattle at last followed the hay onto high ground. '

Constable Booth cycled home to Bradwell mid-morning, cold and exhausted. He was promoted as a result of his outstanding service that night. The houseboat from Mersea had been retrieved.

Enid and John Lodge lived in one of the coastguard cottages just 20 yards from the sea wall. Enid remembers the 1953 floods at the Waterside, Bradwell-on-Sea, very well:

' It was bitterly cold, the wind whistling and roaring around the six Old Coastguard Cottages where we lived in number 3 with our 18-month-old son. The baby woke us up at 1 a.m. that night; my husband got up to see to him and said, 'It's almost daylight outside, the moon's so bright!' Then there was a loud knocking and shouting at our back door. It was a neighbour and a police officer who said, 'The sea wall is breached and the water is coming in all ways – save what you can and stay upstairs'. Upstairs we watched the water coming in the front and back door and creeping up the stairs. My Mum and Dad lived at number 5 and Grandma, aged 90, at number 6. There was a door upstairs connecting Mum's house and Gran's so they at least could have a cup of tea. Grandma slept through the night and refused to move out afterwards, saying, 'Old Hitler never got me out, nor will the sea!'

The wall had been breached behind the house, and overtopped at the front. At dawn we came downstairs to ankle-deep mud and an awful smell. I opened the oven door and the beef joint I had put in the night before floated out on dirty seawater, so I said, 'Salt beef for dinner today!' In fact, all those who had been flooded out took their meat to the local shop where the three sisters who ran it, Melba, Joan and Hilda, cooked Sunday dinner for everyone. Most people went to the Green Man or the little shop overnight, but we went to mum-in-law's.

On Monday morning we went back to hose down the walls and furniture, shovel out mud and light fires to start drying out. John took the day off his work at the local blacksmith's and lost a day's pay because of it! It was weeks before it dried and the smell went. The damp continued to come through the wallpaper for years until John lined the walls with Polystyrene. The lovely piano accordion my Dad had bought me for my 21st birthday had disintegrated but I eventually received £25 compensation for it. The good Canadian people sent us a red carpet (first one we ever had) and a fluffy blanket. The following week, my Mother and I helped to fill sandbags to plug the sea wall. **'**

A distance away from the village, near the chapel of St Peter-on-the-Wall, is a small brick and timber marshman's cottage, formerly the home of Bill Linnett. Bill's grandfather first settled there after retiring from the Navy, and in 1953 Bill's parents still lived at the cottage with him, the old man being 79 and his wife 83. Bill had previously worked for famers on the sea wall, and in 1953 he worked for the River Board.

On the night of the floods, Bill came home after having his Saturday pint at the Cricketers Arm's in Bradwell, leaving about 10.30 p.m. There had been little ebb in the afternoon, it was very cold and Bill could hardly stand in the high wind. He had warned people in the pub that there would be a high tide, but nobody listened. At about 11.15 p.m. he walked along the wall a few hundred yards from the cottage to the concrete Pill Box. The tide was rising high over the saltings and as he watched, a great wave of water, several feet high, rushed towards the walls. He hurried back to the

The chapel of St Peter-on-the-Wall, Bradwell. (Sue Wallace)

cottage and woke his father, who then walked up to the farm to telephone the River Board. After this first rush of water there appeared to be an ebb, which Bill associated afterwards with flooding at Jaywick. Then another rush of water came in, up to the top of the walls and over, and seeing the force and height of the water he said to his mother, 'They walls will have to let goo' [*sic*]. Again, there seemed to be an ebb before the water rushed forward for a third time, overtopping the walls and pouring inland over the flat ground, looking in the moonlight 'like a sheet of glass'. About midnight there was a sound like 'a clap of thunder' as the walls 'let go' at Eastlands. Again, his elderly father set out along the bleak and windswept track to the farm to report that the 'walls had let go'. But all the engineers were out and the foreman had gone to Steeple and Bradwell village to call out the wall walkers.

At about 6 a.m., while it was still dark, Bill started out to walk his stretch of wall down to the Howe Outfall. He had not gone very far when, looking back, he saw a light following him. It was the very welcome light of his colleague Jim Rush, sent by his foreman to walk the wall with him as it was safer for two. On the wall they had to negotiate breaches down to salting level with the water pouring through them, and stretches of wall where the landward side was scoured away and would collapse under a man's weight. The two got back at about 10 a.m. and began to clear the

The sea attacked from the front and the rear of the coastguards' cottages,
by the sea wall at Bradwell. (Courtesy of Enid Lodge)

sluices of debris and silt. The crosscurrents of water pouring through the breaches and churning like a witches cauldron shifted obstacles in every conceivable direction; cattle tanks from the farm were sucked outwards towards the walls, to where a digger was submerged to within 2 feet of the top of the cab. Bill reported on the unusual wave action. The water rose steadily over the saltings until the great waves came with their peculiar after-ebbs, but Linnett's cottage is in a sheltered hollow on slightly raised ground and was not flooded.

Tom Driberg, the MP for Maldon, stayed in his house in Bradwell for the time it took for the walls to be repaired. He became a temporary wall walker, daily checking and recording conditions on his allotted one-and-a-half mile length of wall. On Sunday, 15 February he noted, 'All quiet, water gently lapping base of wall. Home to bed 3.30 a.m.'

Bradwell folk commented on the extreme helpfulness and efficiency of Americans – men of the Texan USAF. Nothing was too much trouble for them and they freely offered all the help they could give in the way of transport, labour and equipment. The easy-going Americans, working vigorously in the clinging mud alongside the Scots and Life Guards on the Bradwell sea walls, were amazed that the Guards were immaculate at all times. They discovered, however, that the Guardsmen were also highly efficient.

For relaxation the military men joined the locals in the pubs, where one remarked, 'Dead tired as they were after long days on the muddy wall, they managed a song of an evening. One Scots Guardsman enlivened the Green Man with "The March of the Cameron Men" and another, a poem about a camel, of which the less said the better'.

13

ALTHORNE AND HOCKLEY

The North Sea surge continued its inexorable course down the Dengie peninsula and unabated up the River Crouch to Battlesbridge, flooding villages and farms on route. Mr Boardman, of Lunts Farm in Paglesham, was the first to alert the police, phoning early on Sunday to report that the wall had been breached and the whole area flooded. Southminster farmer, David Fisher, met floodwater advancing up the road towards his farm that morning, with hares running in front. David was put in charge of repairing the 120-foot wide 'vile breach' at Norpits on the opposite bank of the Crouch. The task was to fill the breach before the next high tide. At one stage, after hours of backbreaking toil, when the wall was almost built, the sea burst through again and 'in a second' hurled a punt with three men on it, from the seaward side of the breach, through the gap and into the field. 'Luckily the men stayed inside. We had to wait till the next low tide to start again.'

Peter Corton and his wife imagined no danger from the sea, in their caravan home at the Dome Country Club in Hockley. But the club was dangerously near the 'vile breach' and the site was overwhelmed by midnight. Woken by neighbours, the dazed and horrified couple stepped out into seawater up to their necks. Their baby daughter in her carrycot was held above Peter's head until they reached the safety of the Club House.

A member of the WVS recorded her memories of the sea wall breach at Althorne: 'Sixty men came from London to repair it. They worked in dreadful conditions at all hours, and could be approached only over flooded fields and by climbing hedges'. The women of Althorne organised themselves to provide hot soup daily for the workers:

' We borrowed large pressure cookers and thermos carriers from Burnham County School and had the carriers fitted with webbing straps so they could be carried on the back.

Material for the soup was obtained partly from our gardens or the rabbit warrens on farms. We also had outside donors: Dunmow bacon factory gave us bones and pigs' trotters: Poultry Packers Ltd, of Wickford, gave second class chickens: The International Stores helped, as did some London butchers and Mr Williams of our local shop. The material was so rich and plentiful that our soup was a meal in itself.

Men working on the sea wall at Tillingham line up for a hot meal. The horse and cart which delivered the meal waits. (Courtesy of Women's Royal Voluntary Services)

We transported the soup to the station and then men carried it to the workers at the wall. In doing this we very much appreciated the help of Mr Turner, the stationmaster, and his staff. There was no difficulty in getting volunteers, and we worked together cheerfully and to the best of our abilities. The men were as grateful for the food as we were to them for mending the breach. '

14

BURNHAM-ON-CROUCH, FOULNESS AND HAVENGORE

Val Cross, a young resident of Burnham-on-Crouch in 1953, later recalled Dr Ben Light's house – which backed onto the sea wall at the end of the High Street – and all houses between the wall and the High Street, being flooded to a depth of 4 feet. In the 1970s, electrician Roger Osborne grazed his hand on a wall in the house, and, licking the graze, was amazed to taste the salt from the 1953 flood.

But away from the harbour, most people on that Sunday morning were unaware that part of their town had been flooded, that twenty-four people were temporarily homeless, or that their island neighbours on Foulnesss and Wallasea were submerged.

Roy Richmond was a 12-year-old member of St Mary's Church choir when, at the end of the morning service, the vicar announced that all members of organisations such as the WVS or St John Ambulance should report to the lower end of Burnham because it was flooded. Roy wrote:

' I went home to tell my family, but Dad had already gone to fill sandbags. I put on my Sea Scout uniform and wellingtons and walked down to Coronation Road, where water was halfway up my legs. At the harbour, local people and Army and RAF personnel were working on a large breach in the sea wall next to the Crouch Yacht Club.

I was joined by other scouts, including my mate Morris Halliday. People were worrying about the shortage of sand to fill the much-needed sandbags, so eight of us went to the local iron foundry in Foundry Lane and loaded the black sand we found there into sacks and onto lorries.

The police directed us to a large breach on the east side of the Royal Corinthian Yacht Club and with locals and members of the armed forces, we worked for hours. As we worked, looking due south the whole area was one massive lake of water as far as the eye could see and across the water the only sign of life was a line of cows on top of the Wallasea wall, silhouetted against the sky.

At about an hour before the next high tide, the work speeded up and suddenly with about fifteen minutes to go, it went deadly quiet. Then a maroon flare was fired above our heads exactly at high tide. Our wall repair had held. Everybody shouted and cheered. '

Repairing the breach on the sea wall at Burnham. (Courtesy of Kevin Bruce)

On the south bank of the Crouch, opposite Burnham, the islands of Wallasea, Foulness, Havengore, Potton, Rushley and New England are separated from each other by the many creeks of the Crouch. These remote estuarine islands, set in the Essex coastal marshes, were largely formed from reclaimed grazing marshland in medieval times. On Foulness, the largest of the islands, there are two small villages, Churchend and Courtsend.

The island's population in 1953 was between 250 and 300. Foulness has been controlled by the military for many years and is used as a testing ground for munitions.

Mr Burroughs, who farmed Rugwood Farm on Foulness, in his detailed account of events that night, recorded that a northerly gale had been blowing all day:

' Although gales were by no means rare, this particular one did seem worse than usual, and we went to bed that night to the sound of roaring wind, rattling doors and window frames. I was awakened about one o'clock in the morning and, looking out of the window, I saw the wind moving the water, and realised the tide had broken through. When I got outside I could hear the animals – cows, sheep and pigs – calling but I could not reach any of them, as the land was lower away from the house, and the water waist-deep. My foreman, who lived in a cottage 200 yards away from the farmhouse, appeared at a window with a torch, but we had to wait till daylight before we could do anything. '

Churchfields, Foulness. In the foreground, Henry Hume can just be seen carrying his son, Trevor, to the waiting boat. (Courtesy of Foulness Heritage Centre)

Mr Burroughs of Rugwood Farm, Foulness, surveys his flooded fields. He had lost many head of cattle, but his family were safe. (Courtesy of John Threadgold)

Everywhere on the island, people of this largely farming community were woken by the sound of water too near to their homes, and the sound of terrified animals.

When daylight came, Mr Burroughs saw

‘ … one vast expanse of water, with only a few trees and haystacks visible. The wind was still very strong and the weather very cold. From the bedroom windows we could see the gaps in the sea wall where the water had broken through. Floating about on the water were bales of hay and straw, chicken houses, and even a car.

As I could not get to the yards where the animals were, I called to my foreman to open the gates, but the water was too deep. He could not hear anything of them so he looked from a bedroom window and saw that the eighteen cattle in one yard were drowned.

Deciding I must do something about the cattle in the other yard I made myself a raft, and managed to get as far as a tractor shed, near the cattle yard, when the raft capsized. I was already wet to the waist so I decided to walk through the water, but the force of the wind and water was too strong for me to open the gate. By this time the foreman had also arrived at the tractor shed and started one of the tractors. When he backed it out, however, it went into deep water and would go no further.

I then saw my horseman, who had waded from the village along the main road, and had tried to get across to where the horses were in their stable. The water was too deep and we'd lost them. He was forced to turn back, very distressed. Shouting to me that he would come back later, he returned home. ’

In the island cottages people helped each other as much as possible. Most of the men had rubber thigh boots and could wade from house to house. Fires were lit in bedrooms, and where no coal or wood was available children's toys and old gramophone records were used for fuel.

The depth of the water varied considerably over the island. Those whose homes were nearest the sea walls, particularly in the north of the island, suffered the full force of the water as it broke through these walls. On this reclaimed land the water lay trapped for weeks between the old sea walls. But these walls were now roads, and though flooded, facilitated some movement of traffic.

At Foulness Point, soon after 1 a.m. on Sunday, the sea burst through the wall in eight places, leaving just 60 yards of wall standing in a mile. Mr W. Rawlings, a retired Metropolitan Police Sergeant, was living in a cottage at Courtsend, near Ridgemarsh Farm. At about 2 a.m. he saw 'huge waves in the River Crouch, much above sea level'. About an hour later there was 18 inches of water in his kitchen. Outside, water was rushing down the road, north to south, and at the sea wall he could see an avalanche of water crashing through the gaps onto the island.

Mr Rawlings' sister-in-law, 64-year-old Bertha Rawlings, lived in a small timber cottage just yards from the sea wall at Crouch Corner. With the surge at its height and most dangerous, Mr Rawlings set out towards her home. To avoid being swept away, he hooked himself with a boathook to anything at hand and was able to wake the occupants of cottages as he went.

But the water nearer the wall was too deep and the current too strong. He made three attempts to reach the cottage during the night and at last, as the tide ebbed at about 6 a.m., he succeeded in rescuing a teacher from Barling School, who lived next door to Bertha, but he did not find his sister-in-law.

The children of Foulness, returning in the howling wind from a Sunday school party at Churchend, had met Bertha Rawlings on the road that afternoon. She said she was going home for a 'nice cup of tea and to get warm'. When the water burst into their homes the teacher was trapped, unable to open the door against the weight of water. Bertha went for help and was swept away. Her neighbour survived.

Bertha was still missing on 4 February when the ex-policeman told a *Daily Sketch* reporter: 'My sister-in-law is in the fields ahead, she died trying to reach me.' Her body was recovered from Fisherman's Head two weeks later, on Sunday, 14 February, by PC James Blackhurst, who described the incident: 'We arrived at Ridgemarsh Farm, Courtsend, to look for Mrs Bertha Rawlings. When I was about half a mile away from Ridgemarsh Farm, I saw her body. She was lying on her back in about 6 inches of water and was partly dressed'. Very deep, flood-filled ditches each side of the old sea wall on which he stood, prevented the constable from reaching the body until a number of military personnel arrived to help.

Mrs Rawlings' son was shown his mother's clothing in order to identify the body. She had been with him on Foulness on 29 January, and he had not seen her since. There had been 7 feet of water at Courtsend.

Violet Rawlings (no relation of Bertha), a widow aged 41, lived on Foulness with her elderly mother and two children. Derek Shuttlewood, a young islander, set out early on Sunday morning along flooded roads to Violet's isolated bungalow at Fisherman's Head. There he was told that Violet had left the house to get help, but 'had been washed away'. Derek carried the children, one a young baby, over the plank 'bridge' across the flooded ditch and home to his mother, before returning for the grandmother, who also needed to be carried. Violet's body was found some distance from her home on Monday and, as rescuers concentrated on the living, 9-year-old Ruth Nicholls, passing in a rescue boat, was troubled by the sight of Violet's body lying in a handcart.

By daylight on Sunday morning, concern for the people of Foulness had grown considerably. There had been no communication with the island. Fishermen, boatmen and farmers, worried about friends and relatives living there, began attempts to cross the river in small boats, but the raging water prevented passage. Harry Willsmer, marooned on Foulness, rode a 'calm old farm horse', towards Great Wakering to get help, but at the dam the water was so deep that the horse began to swim. Harry, a non-swimmer, did a u-turn towards home.

Meanwhile, the police, fire brigade and HM Coastguard were standing by till attempts could be made to cross, and both Burnham-on-Crouch and Great Wakering were preparing reception centres for the evacuees.

The army sent a DUKW (an amphibian vehicle) to Great Wakering on Sunday morning to try to get across to Foulness via the only (now flooded) road from the mainland, but at Havengore Bridge it ran into hidden obstacles below the water and had to be abandoned and the crew brought back to dry land.

The high tide in the early afternoon on Sunday caused even more devastation to the islands, with water in some parts rising again to 8 feet. At this time, a Gemini aircraft from Southend Municipal airport made a reconnaissance flight over the whole of the Thames estuary area. The pilot telephoned the manager on return and reported that 'no signs of life' had been seen on Foulness.

By 4.30 p.m. there had still been no contact with the island; the police report at the time states briefly, 'Whole island under 6 feet of water – no contact – concern for 150-200 villagers'. With everyone becoming more and more anxious a second attempt was made to get from Great Wakering across the flooded road to Foulness. In the late afternoon, with light fading, Sergeant Harrison set out in another DUKW. At Havengore, he and his crew rescued the bridge keeper and his family and took them back to dry land. But, on the return journey, the vehicle strayed off road into deep water and the men found they could neither get over nor through the breached sea wall. Seeing lights flashing from a house nearby, the crew went to their aid and managed to get the occupants back to the stranded DUKW. However, when they went to pull off, wire had become caught all round the body and wheels and the vehicle was completely stuck. Rescued and rescuers spent the bitterly cold night keeping warm by square dancing on the few feet of the DUKW deck. There they stayed till about 9 a.m. on Monday, when rescued by Leigh fishermen. The DUKW was not recovered until several days later.

The Gemini aircraft from Southend went out again just before nightfall for a specific survey of Foulness. This time the pilot reported he had seen a military policeman on a roof, a man in a boat, and a few people at upstairs windows signalling to him.

On Sunday evening, as the day drew to a close and darkness set in, many said that if contact with the people could not be made in the daylight, it was certain nothing could be done during the hours of darkness.

Six of the War Department Constables patrolling the island had gathered together as conditions worsened, but War Department Sergeant Stanley Gray was alone at 11.50 p.m. on Saturday when he telephoned headquarters from Havengore Bridge. Foulness teenager Roy Ducker, returning from a dance at Great Wakering, met the constable at the bridge when the water flowing over it was level with the handrail. Roy decided to return to the mainland, but Sergeant Gray said he would go to warn the stockman at nearby Havengore Farm. At the farm, the stockman, once woken, drove the cattle out of the cowshed, although at that time there was no water near the farmhouse.

A moment later the two men saw a wall of water coming towards them over the railway line, and from the west, another huge wave approaching. The stockman hurried indoors to get his family upstairs. Sergeant Gray went to a building on Havengore Island, known as Taylor's Hut, and reported to headquarters that the water had reached the farm but that the occupants were safe. It was the last message he was able to send.

The occupiers of the farm on Havengore Island later reported seeing Sergeant Gray on the roof of the two-storied Taylor's Hut. The Southend pilot had seen him there too. He survived the icy cold night alone on the roof, and on Sunday morning he was seen from the upstairs windows of a house a few hundred yards away, trying to wade through the rough and deep water back to Foulness. The police reported that he must have wandered off the submerged road and been swept off his feet, and though normally a strong swimmer, weakened by the night's exposure, had been washed into the creek.

After constant searches, the body of Sergeant Stanley Gray was recovered almost two months later, on 29 March, in the creek between New England and Havengore Islands. He was 47 years old.

An imaginary sightseer, standing at dawn in Wakering Road on the edge of Great Wakering, and looking out across Havengore, Rushley and New England Islands, and on across Foulness to Foulness Point, would see before them seven miles of unbroken floodwater resembling a very choppy sea. Within this watery landscape, throughout Sunday night, the people of Foulness huddled in their cold and wet bedrooms, listened to the water lapping round their cottages and the cries of their terrified animals, and wondered 'what the morrow would bring?'

Monday morning brought, at last, the rescue force which had been gathering since Sunday morning, waiting for tide and weather to allow them access to the island after thirty hours of silence. At about 2 a.m., a small Thames barge, *Cygnet*, from Little Wakering, manned by its owner 'Gaffer' Mumford and locals from Barling and Little Wakering, sailed down the River Roach on the night tide and anchored off Foulness quay, just before high water. There they waited to begin the work of rescue.

The Southend lifeboat had butted its way to Foulness at 9.30 p.m. on Sunday night, and anchored off Fisherman's Head on the other side of the island. Before dawn, her searchlights could be seen making sweeps of the walls, looking for gaps through which to haul small boats. And at first light fishermen from Paglesham, who had been standing by all day Sunday, set off for Foulness.

Soon, the first families were collected from near East Newlands Farm on the mouth of the River Crouch by the Southend lifeboat, and were taken across the hazardous stretch of water to the rest centre at Burnham-on-Crouch.

Foulness Quay with the sea on both sides of the wall. A small barge anchored there overnight, ready for the first evacuations. (Courtesy of John Threadgold)

At last, on 2 February, as the tide was ebbing, more rescue forces were approaching the north and south walls of the island. From Shoebury they drove across the Maplin Sands on the Ancient Broomway – passable only at low tide and dangerous at all times, it had been underwater since Saturday night. Army lorries and those belonging to the Leigh Building Supply Company drove as far as possible onto the island, where 'Gaffer' Mumford with his crew, plus fishermen and volunteers from Leigh and all nearby places, collected people from their flooded homes, helped them into their boats and rowed them to the waiting lorries. Evacuees were taken by lorry back across the sands, first to Shoebury garrison, where they were given tea and biscuits, and then on to Great Wakering, where a reception and rest centre had been set up.

At Rugwood Farm, at about 8.30 a.m. on Monday, Mr Burroughs and his family were relieved to see the Paglesham fishermen rowing their boats into the farmyard. Mrs Burroughs and the children were helped into a fishing boat – the 15-month-old twins were happy and excited, but the two older siblings were more aware and scared. Mr Burroughs and his parents watched anxiously from an upstairs window until the fishing boats were out of sight.

Mr Burroughs said, 'Later my wife told me that it was a frightening journey, and they were all very cold before they were halfway to the sea wall, but the fishermen were wonderful and somehow found a way through barbed wire and gateposts and all the floating debris. They eventually arrived at the sea wall and were taken by motorboat to Burnham-on-Crouch, where they were wonderfully treated by members of WVS, Salvation Army, St John Ambulance and other voluntary services.'

At Burnham-on-Crouch, opposite Foulness to the north, the Royal Corinthian Yacht Club had been fully prepared to receive the evacuees since Sunday, knowing that the islanders had been marooned for almost thirty hours. Dr Annette Wyatt, from Maldon, waiting to play her part, watched as the 'little Dunkirk fleet of every available kind of craft, such as motorboats, oyster-smacks and landing-craft set out for Foulness'.

At last the boats were seen in the distance, returning with rescued passengers, who were helped up the slipway and taken straight into the lounge, while the boats went back for more. A mug of thick hot soup was given to everyone, but most, though cold and

Children rescued from Foulness being carried into the Royal Corinthian Yacht Club at Burnham. (Courtesy of Kevin Bruce)

DUKWs on Foulness. (Mirrorpix)

wet, did not want baths until they knew where their friends and relatives were. Later, they were given a meal of meat and vegetables, with apple pie and custard for pudding.

Dr Wyatt recorded that a newly delivered mother was put straight to bed in a large sunny room, where she was able to breastfeed her baby, and a large quantity of 'destroyable' nappies were provided for her use. Two or three old men refused both a change of clothing and a bath, seeming more afraid of the bath than the floods.

The doctor noted that the outstanding characteristic of the day was selflessness. The islanders were anxious for one another. For some, it was their first time off the island. The islanders enjoyed the attention of professional waiters and stewards and a tot of rum before bed, courtesy of a London member of the club. Everyone praised the 'organising genius' who kept everything going smoothly, the steward of the Corinthian Club, Mr Kit Deacon.

Helpers were intrigued by the contents of the evacuees' sacks, which moved when set aside, but as Roy Ducker later explained, they merely contained their cats. Mary Evelyn Wallace, the Foulness sub-postmistress, however, brought all her GPO stocks of postal orders, stamps and cash. An elderly gentleman clutched a sack containing between £3,000 and £4,000, which he was most reluctant to place in the Club safe, as he 'did not hold with banks'.

Major S.E. Toghill, with Warrant Officers Crossman and Allen, came from Shoebury on Monday morning in a DUKW as part of the evacuation of Foulness. The Major recorded that navigation proved difficult; the DUKW was sometimes afloat and sometimes on its wheels on the ground, and that the only possible way of proceeding was to stand up on the front end and, with a long pole, measure the depth of water as he went along to ensure that the vehicle stayed on the road 'without being shipwrecked'. Wherever they went they saw horses, cattle, sheep, pigs and poultry marooned in unapproachable places. Rabbits huddled together in treetops and hens shared a hummock of grass with a fox!

The most tragic episode the Major saw was the rescue of three sheep, which were seen apparently marooned on a small mound of hay, but it was discovered that the mound on which they were standing was comprised of dead sheep, and that these three were the soul survivors of a panic-stricken flock of fifty sheep.

At Shelford, where the water was 6 feet deep, the six War Department Constables, who had been marooned at their post since Saturday, were found. They were taken aboard the

Rounding up the livestock on Foulness. (Courtesy of Foulness Heritage Centre)

Fifty head of cattle swam half a mile to safety. (Courtesy of John Threadgold)

DUKW and given a very welcome tot of rum and some food. The six men were then taken in the DUKW to look for their comrade, Constable Gray, at Taylor's Hut, where he was last seen – a search which proved futile.

The few hundred people of Foulness lived either in one of the small villages or in outlying farms and homesteads. The little boats worked tirelessly all day, at great risk to themselves, to find and collect the scattered inhabitants and to ferry them across to the sea wall, or sometimes all the way to Great Wakering. By Monday evening very few were left on the island. Representatives of the RSPCA, the press, and a collection of farmers and farm labourers who came to help round up the livestock, remained.

On Tuesday morning, a farmer friend of Mr Burroughs arrived from Southchurch in an army DUKW, and most of the remaining islanders, including the elderly Mr and Mrs Burroughs, were taken across the Broomway to Shoebury. With his parents safe, the farmer concentrated on trying to rescue some of the animals.

Men from William King & Sons, boat builders, joined the animal rescue teams. On one of their rescue trips, Harold Cross put his hand into the water and scooped up a lobster. Val, his daughter, never forgot: 'My parents boiled it in the copper and at 12 years old that was my first taste of the expensive range of shellfish – it was normally winkles, whelks or shrimps for Sunday tea.'

Some creatures, though, were much more difficult to manage. Harold Cross told his future son-in-law, 'You haven't lived, mate, until you've tried to get a cow into a motor launch'.

15

WALLASEA AND CREEKSEA

A young man returning home on his motorbike to Wallasea Island from a dance on the mainland was the first to raise the alarm about the seriousness of the flooding on the island. Mr Freeman met water flowing across the approach road to Wallasea at Lion Creek, which was not unusual, and which he crossed, but from the sea wall which encircles Wallasea he saw that the island was 'as full of water as a dog's bowl'. He could go no further. Anxious about his parents in their bungalow on Wallasea, he returned to the mainland and telephoned his father's employer, Mr Brown, a local farmer.

Mr Brown immediately phoned Mrs Carey of nearby Raymonds Farm. This was about 3 a.m. Colonel and Mrs Carey had also been to a dance that night, in the Delf Café in Rochford. On returning home they went to bed, unaware that the sea had approached to within 100 yards of the house. When Mr Brown telephoned, Mrs Carey looked out of the window at a lake of water surrounding their home.

As a result of repeated requests, Colonel Carey reluctantly got out of bed and, driven on by his wife, was 'persuaded' down to the water's edge with his pram dinghy carried on the back of his A40 pickup. At about 4 a.m. he was pushed off in the dinghy and launched alone onto the waters of Wallasea Island by friends Brown and Groom, being requested by Mr Brown to try to locate the Freeman family in a bungalow near the old Creeksea Ferry Inn. It was dark – visibility was about 50 yards – and the wind was very strong.

Mrs Ivy Taylor-Smith, the licensee of the Creeksea Ferry Inn, just 20 yards behind the sea wall, was, at that time, perilously close to death by drowning, exhaustion, exposure or shock. After supporting herself by hanging onto the top of a door, in water up to her neck, for nearly seven hours, she had almost lost the will to live. Colonel Carey, reluctant though he was to get out of his warm bed, saved her life and became a hero that night.

There is more than one account of what happened that night at the Creeksea Ferry Inn. Certainly, there were only three customers left in the pub at closing time – Charles Rolfe, Dick Whitworth and Harry Wheeler. Between 11.30 and midnight the three customers and Ivy went out to look at the water, which was nearly up to the top of the sea wall. At some time late in the evening, the nightwatchman of the Davey and Armitage timber yard on Wallasea cycled to the inn and warned the landlady and her three customers about the expected high tide, before going to his own bungalow nearby.

Soon, water was seeping into the pub lounge and within minutes it was sloshing around their knees. Mrs Taylor-Smith telephoned her friend in Thorpe Bay and her friend telephoned the police, who recorded the call. In one account Ivy then, 'tried to make a dash for it with the three men, and though the car started, it stalled after a few yards and they all waded back to the inn'. In another, 'the three men left to return to Canewdon and Rochford by car and Ivy locked up for the night. Then, at Lion Creek, the men found the tide flowing over the road, and the water too deep to drive through, so they returned to the inn. Ivy welcomed them back, told them it would probably be an hour or so before the tide ebbed enough for them to cross, and gave them coffee and pork pies while they waited'. Whichever was the case, back in the pub, they all decided to climb out of the lounge window onto the flat roof. Two of the men went up while Ivy went to find a coat (she was wearing a thin 'little black dress'), Charles Rolfe guiding her with a torch. Then, suddenly, a wall of water came crashing down the passage leading to the cellar and blocked their way. Mrs Taylor-Smith later told the *Daily Sketch*:

‘ We jumped on the kitchen table, hoping that at any moment the level would stop rising, but soon it covered the table and was lifting it up. Everything was floating around – furniture, cups and saucers, glasses. We couldn't reach the window. Charles had a torch and said he was going to swim for help. I told him not to be silly, but he wanted to go, and the last time I saw him he was swimming away with the torch in his hand. The police found him, drowned, still clutching the torch. ’

Ivy, now alone, put her foot on the kitchen door latch and hung with all her strength onto the top of the door. 'There were things floating around my head and I kept telling myself to keep my wits about me and hang onto the door. I thought it was never going to end, and perhaps I'd better let go and die. But as soon as I thought that I would get angry and say to myself – No! I have so many things in life still to do.'

Colonel Carey, on his lonely mission to find the trapped Freeman family, passed the Creeksea Ferry Inn just before daylight. He had rowed alone in the dark, against the howling wind, past breaches in the sea wall from which gushing water swept him off course; a heroic feat. At the pub he saw two men standing on the roof. They told him that Mrs Taylor-Smith was still inside, but they thought that another man had been drowned. It was now about 5 a.m. The Colonel rowed round the back of the pub, broke the window with his oar and climbed down from the dinghy into the flooded room, where the water was up to his chest. There he saw Mrs Taylor-Smith hanging onto the door. He helped her down, carried her to the window and the two men on the roof got her into the boat and rowed her over to the sea wall. From there, wrapped in a fisherman's jumper, she was rowed across the fields of Wallasea and finally taken to Rochford Hospital, where she was admitted at 9 a.m. on Sunday, 1 February, her ordeal finally over.

The body of 43-year-old Charles Rolfe was found in the same room later in the day, when the police searched the pub. He had drowned.

The Colonel then continued his rescue mission, heading for the Freeman's bungalow. Earlier that evening, the Essex River Board engineer had warned the nightwatchman of the timber yard that there would be a flood and, in water up to his knees, he cycled home, warning Mrs Taylor-Smith at the inn on the way. The nightwatchman collected his wife and neighbours, including the Freemans, from their bungalows near the sea wall, and together they waded through 4 feet of fast-flowing water to a loft in the farm building, where they spent the night. In the morning, when Colonel Carey reached them, he advised that they wait in safety for a larger boat.

In the early hours of Sunday, Colonel Carey was the sole rescuer out and about with a boat in Wallasea. After leaving the Freemans he noticed lights flashing at Grapnells Farm, about three-quarters of a mile further on, and rowed in that direction. On the way he ferried two more people from the Wallasea Bay Yacht Club over to the sea wall. At Grapnells, on the highest point on the island, water had risen to 2 feet in the downstairs rooms, and had reached the bellies of the cows in the stalls. But the Wheals, of Grapnells Farm, an old marsh family, were not unduly concerned. They welcomed the Colonel, by now wet and very cold, put him to bed while his clothes dried and 'brought him up a hearty hot breakfast on a tray'.

After breakfast, Colonel Carey walked to the mainland at low water, along the broken top of the sea wall, leaving his dinghy with the farmer at Grapnells in case he should need it. He telephoned the police at Burnham and Rochford, informing them of the true position at Wallasea and advised them to begin rescue operations from Burnham. Then, as soon as the tide ebbed far enough, Rochford police and people from the mainland waded across Lion Creek to the island wall and the first people were brought out and taken to hospital before noon.

Rising tide and fierce wind made it impossible to continue the rescue operation until mid-afternoon, but by 4 p.m. ten people had been rescued and the body of Charles Rolfe recovered from the Creeksea Ferry Inn. By nightfall, thanks to volunteers from the Canewdon and Burnham districts, the Burnham and Rochford Police and Essex County and Southend ambulances, the only people left on Wallasea, of the population of thirty-seven, were the six members of the Wheal family at Grapnells Farm, who preferred to remain.

All day Sunday, 3 feet or more of water remained cupped inside the island. Hilda Grieve, in her book *The Great Tide*, describes the view wonderfully:

' Fences were completely covered and the ebbing tide had left the telegraph wires festooned with fluttering ribbons of seaweed and wisps of grass. In one bungalow a table with an oil lamp on it had floated up to the ceiling, crushed the funnel against it and floated down again, leaving a black ring imprinted above. The cab of a River Board excavator was submerged to the jib, which broke the surface like the neck of a giraffe out for a swim. The exhaust funnel of a bulldozer, just poking through, might have been a submarine snorkel. As the second tide rose, more water flowed in through the gaps in the wall. '

Repairs to a sea wall. (Reuter's image, reproduced courtesy of Essex Record Office)

An auxiliary postman, James Burns, aged 70, attached to Burnham sub office, resided on Wallasea and delivered the rural post on the island. On Saturday evening he returned from the mainland at 10 p.m., collected his bicycle and changed back into his wellington boots at the Wallasea Bay café. As he left the café to set out for his bungalow at Allfleets a couple of miles away, he remarked, 'I expect I shall have to walk home with all this wind'. No one will ever know the horror of his homeward journey. His body was recovered about six weeks later, on 8 March, from the Delf ditch behind the sea wall. At his bungalow nearby, there was evidence (seaweed and grass) that the water had reached the ceiling.

The position on the remote Potton Island with its single farm was still unknown to officials at 4 p.m. on Sunday, but the farm tenants had been rescued by their employers on the midday tide, with the exception of an elderly couple who refused to leave. Later, 'Gaffer' Mumford and others from Wakering and Barling, on the island to rescue sheep, persuaded them to return to the mainland with them in the barge, *Cygnet*.

In 1953, Mr Bob Crosby was a member of a small group of bachelors working at Marconi's in Chelmsford, who had formed themselves into a club. When the floods occurred they decided, as a group, to go and help, and the postmaster at Great Baddow, where Mr Crosby lived, organised a party and arranged a coach. They had to bring their own spades and shovels. Bob knew he had gone somewhere near Canewdon on the first Sunday after the floods, and only later learned that he was actually working on Wallasea Island. The effect of the flooding was such that he had not the least idea that he was on an island.

16

GREAT
WAKERING

Great Wakering is a village approximately four miles east of Southend and about a mile inland from the Thames estuary and the Maplin Sands. In 1953, according to the Meteorological Office, it had the lowest rainfall in England.

On the Common, at the edge of the village, thirty-seven families had temporary homes in semi-circular Nissen huts, which had formally been used to house prisoners of war. The homes provided independence for young couples with children, who were awaiting the allocation of council houses. All main services were connected, and each home had a kitchen, bathroom, lavatory and a small garden. The estate, known as Home Farm Camp, was situated a quarter of a mile south of the tidal Mill Head Creek, which was surrounded by sea walls.

The drowned Nissen huts on Great Wakering Common on 2 February, when the water level was considerably lower. (Courtesy of John Threadgold)

PC Griffiths alerted the village of Great
Wakering. (Courtesy of Peter Griffiths)

On 1 February, at about 1 a.m., the tide overtopped the wall at Morrins Point, below Wakering Stairs, and began a stealthy and silent advance across the New Ranges towards the Nissen huts and their sleeping occupants.

A young man, Mr Finch, was returning home from a dance at the village hall when, at the end of the lane leading to the common, he saw the water creeping towards the huts. He rushed back towards the village and by chance met the local constable, PC Griffiths, near the church. They both returned to the common in ankle-deep water. After warning his parents, the youth joined the constable to awaken the occupants of the huts.

A few of the younger residents were persuaded to wade through the water carrying their children, and, following PC Griffiths, they reached the village.

The constable then went to the fire station to get help and, finding the electricity had failed and the alarm was dead, he cycled to the home of nearest fireman, Mr Hayward, and told him to get a team together and go to the Common.

Cycling on to Cupids Corner, Griffiths met deep floodwater. He roused the occupants there and at Victoria Drive, before continuing towards the High Street. In the High Street he telephoned county police headquarters to report the situation and there met a soaked and exhausted group of Home Farm tenants coming towards him from the Common.

The constable continued round the village, calling out to those who owned boats, and, with members of the fire brigade, began organising rescue operations, before returning to the Common.

There the situation was about to change dramatically. Frederick George was probably the last to make his own way to safety that night. At 2 a.m. he was woken by the sound of water gurgling 6 inches below his windowsill. Frederick managed to force the door open against the rising tide and carried his wife, then his son, to safety through deep but calm water, calling out to his neighbours as he went.

Seconds later the wall at Morris Point was breached. The sea thundered through a gap 180 yards across and surged towards the huts. No one then dared venture into the maelstrom. In a very short time the camp, which stood on very low lying ground, was in water 8 feet deep and the huts impossible to reach.

Unable to open the doors at the front or rear of their homes, the remaining tenants were trapped. Most swiftly made the decision that the roof offered their only chance of survival, and either climbed out of the window and up, or bashed a hole in the roof to struggle through. One elderly couple, Ellen and George Kirby, unable to climb onto the roof, were heard by neighbours singing 'Abide with Me' as they waited and hoped for rescue. Both were later found dead in their home.

Once out in the open whole families clung, in their nightclothes, onto the slippery curved roofs while the wind howled around them, threatening to loosen their precarious hold and drop them into the deep, icy and turbulent water below.

For two young families the night brought heartbreaking tragedy. David and Nellie Whitehead clung onto the roof of their home with their son and daughter for three hours, before Nellie slipped off and was drowned. The rest of the family were rescued and taken to Southend General Hospital. Four-year-old David showed signs of life on admittance but did not recover, despite all attempts by the doctors to save him. He died from shock and exposure on 1 February. The body of his 24-year-old mother was recovered from the Home Farm site on 3 February.

The body of Stuart Curtis, aged 3½, was also not recovered until 3 February. His father, a steeplejack, had been working in Chester and returned to identify the body of his son. The *Essex Weekly News* reported on 6 February that Mrs Mary Curtis had been on the roof with her son, and, when a table top floated by, she saw a way of saving herself and her child. Numbed with cold she placed the terrified child on the makeshift raft, but within seconds, as she tried to clamber on beside him, a wave swept the raft and child out of her grasp. She never saw him again.

By 2.40 a.m., the Wakering firemen had reached the lane leading to the Common but the water was too deep for the appliances to get near the huts, which were, by then, almost completely submerged. Nothing but the curved roofs could be seen above the surface of the water.

While the firemen were attempting to reach the huts, the calls of the tenants were heard by a local brickfield worker, 48-year-old 'Sammy' Sampson. He rowed onto the Common in a 'flattie', just big enough to carry himself, plus one adult and a child. He reached the huts and ferried backwards and forwards, carrying people to safety. It was later estimated that Mr Sampson, working alone, had saved thirty people with one boat.

The reaction of the people of Wakering to the disaster was magnificent, fast and efficient. By 2 a.m. the village was up and ready for action, and the able-bodied were making their way to the Common with their flat-bottomed boats. Mr Johnson and fireman Mr Butler found a boat in the Home Farm yard and rowed with one oar and a broomstick. Les Cripps, the baker, and Ian Rayner, farmer of Home Farm, were rowing to the rescue before 2.30, and by then ambulances were waiting in Churchfields when the first Home Farm tenants were brought off the Common.

To reach the flood victims, in the teeth of the gale, the rescuers had to row across 400-500 yards of rough water in a wind which often swept them past the huts they aimed for. Then, like the rescuers of Jaywick and Harwich, they had to persuade people down from roofs into the rocking boats below, with just one man to steady both boat and terrified passenger. The return journey could take thirty minutes, rowing into the cutting wind. The passengers, in wet nightclothes and frozen to the bone, were handed a welcome tot of whisky by Mr A.H. Bentley, licensee of the Red Lion, when they landed.

By 2.15 a.m., neighbours Mrs Rayner and Mrs Arnold had opened their homes at Home Farm and Cottawight. Fires were lit and hot food and drink prepared. The first to be rescued made their way towards the lighted windows where, though homeless, they would at least be safe, warm and dry.

The church, church hall and vicarage were opened by the vicar, Mr Dickenson, and his wife. Flood victims arriving at the church hall were registered by the welfare officer, given drinks and blankets and taken in villagers' cars to the doctor's house. So well organised was the response that by 4 a.m. the doctor's home had been set up as an emergency hospital, run by the doctor's wife, a trained nurse. Mr Greenleaf, the local fishmonger, took those in need of hospital treatment to Southend Hospital in his car. However, after news of the disaster on Canvey Island reached Wakering, only very severe cases were hospitalised.

Those who could be moved on immediately were taken to homes in the village by local people. Mr McAdden, MP for Southend East, and P.G. Cottis, Chair of Rochford Rural District Council, ferried flood victims anywhere in the area. One hundred and twelve people from the camp passed through the rest centre on Sunday.

By 5 a.m. the information centre had been moved to the village hall and was run jointly by members of the local councils. Mrs Elsie Sheridan, a WVS officer, had called on all neighbours for clothes and blankets, and the village people were serving tea.

The troops had not been needed for rescue work, but the Shoebury officer in charge took over and completed a hut to hut search, knocking a hole through each room in each hut to make sure no one was left inside. A young boy was found on tiptoes on a wardrobe. He had survived for seven hours by gasping air through a ventilator shaft in the roof. In another hut, an elderly couple had balanced on the stove, in water up to their chests, for nine hours. Bodies seen in the water were collected on 2 and 3 February.

At Oxenham Farm, the Threadgold family went into action as soon as they saw the state of the tide. Nineteen-year-old John, with his father and George Mead, their cowman, began to move the cattle to a granary, which was 2 feet off the ground when, in John's words, they 'noticed a white wall coming across the fields from the Thames, where about 100 yards of seawall had been swept away as though made of paper.' He continues:

' The water started to rise rapidly and when it was about waist-deep, Dad shouted to get back to the house, quick! As we went I realised that the cows were still tied up in the cowshed, so I diverted and undid all the yokes and released them. Then I tried to open the big sliding door but there was so much weight of water outside that I couldn't move it. I had to climb over the cows to get back to the small door and out. The animals could not be saved. One of our ponies, Patsy, took a wrong turn, went into the cowshed and she too was drowned. She used to frequently swim to Rushley of her own accord but that didn't help her.

We made our way back to the house, which is the highest part of the farm, and all eleven of us were marooned; five of us, five of the Mead family, plus Uncle Frank Briggs, who had come down from Landwick to give us a hand.

As it got light on Sunday morning we looked out and could see for the first time the total devastation. As far as you could see there was water everywhere. We saw a weak calf fall off the seawall into the water and just give up. On the wall were two cows and Blossom, one of the horses who was heavily in foal.

At breakfast time the one thing missing was breakfast, so I pulled myself round to the kitchen by means of the picture rail and reached for a bowl of dripping and a loaf of bread, which went down very well. My young brother Roy tried his hand at fishing from the stairs with an empty camera case tied on the end of a piece of string, without much success.

Some cattle found a refuge in the old house on Rushley Island. (Courtesy of John Threadgold)

Oxenham Farm, with the family at the window and 'Gaffer'
Mumford in the boat. (Courtesy of John Threadgold)

As the tide came up in the afternoon so the wind increased and we saw the henhouse crumple and float away. Then a landing craft came round the creek, and a rowing boat with 'Gaffer' Mumford and two men was put over the seawall and rowed round to the front of the house. With the bows in the front porch they threw a rope to us with which we lowered everyone down into the boat. When Mrs Mead was being lowered she caught her elastic knicker leg on the window catch, and there she dangled until being pulled up again and released   .

Once on the seawall we could see all the dead animals littered round the buildings, seventy-four in total. At 'Gaffer's' house we had a nice hot cup of tea before going on to our temporary digs.

The next day we, with farmworkers, made our way to Rushley Island to get the young stock that were round the old house. To our surprise, all twenty-nine were alive but in desperate need of fresh water and food. We encouraged them to go through the water to the seawall by walking in front with a truss of hay. Once there we drove them through the creek but the sticky mud took its toll on the weakest, and two got really stuck and had to be left as we needed to guide the others, plus the two cows and the horse, on a long and difficult trek to one of Millbank's meadows. We went back the next day to collect the other two. One had been floated out by the incoming tide and had got to dry land, but the other was too weak and was drowned.

Two months after the flood, Blossom gave birth to twin foals. It is very rare that horses have twins but to have them both survive is almost unheard of, and especially after an ordeal like the flood.

Samuel's Corner, Great Wakering, looking towards Foulness. (Courtesy of John Threadgold)

By 11 a.m. on Sunday, all Great Wakering survivors were being cared for, but it was known that Foulness Island was completely flooded and that nothing had been heard from residents. The Great Wakering rest centres were on standby to receive evacuees.

At midnight that Sunday, the Southend lifeboats attempted the relief of Foulness from the sea, and at 2 a.m. 'Gaffer' Mumford and crew sailed across by moonlight in the barge, *Cygnet*. When rescue proved impossible by night, both teams anchored off Foulness to begin their mission at first light. At 9.30 a.m. on Monday, 2 February, the first lorry-load of people arrived from Foulness via the Broomway. Their clothes were filthy as they had waited or waded where sewage pipes had burst. Mrs Rayner, president of the local WVS, and her team washed and ironed everything.

Some Foulness survivors were first taken to Burnham, and were transferred to Great Wakering by road between 2 and 4 February. A register of village people willing to house them was made and Foulness islander David Rippengale, years later, still remembered the kindness of the Great Wakering people who took them unhesitatingly into their homes. Mr Moorhouse, the owner of the Kursaal in Southend, sent coal to all villagers who took in flood victims, and the school canteen provided a midday meal in the school dining hall.

Two more deaths occurred in the village. Forty-year-old William Driscoll had chronic bronchitis and suffered a heart attack when his home at No. 3 Landwick Cottages was flooded, and 67-year-old Walter Manning, a coal merchant of New Road, also suffering from bronchitis, died of shock and exposure after immersion in floodwater.

Mr Edward 'Gaffer' Mumford received the British Empire Medal for his services during the floods in Essex.

17

SOUTHEND-ON-SEA AND LEIGH-ON-SEA

The cold and windy weather had no impact on peoples' plans for the evening, and at the end of the long Southend Pier, a party of Canvey Islanders were enjoying a dance. The pier officer on duty, however, was not happy with state of the tide, and at 10 p.m. had informed the coastguard and Southend Police of the abnormally high water level. Police cars with public address equipment warned residents just before the water flooded over The Esplanade, Marine Parade and Victoria Road. Six hundred Southend houses were flooded. It was 11.30 p.m.

The only known photograph taken on the night of the flood. It shows the speedway track in Peter Pan's Playground, by the pier. Note the height of water in relation to the 'WAY OUT' sign. (Southend Standard image, reproduced courtesy of Essex Record Office)

No trains at Leigh-on-Sea railway station. (Courtesy of Southend-on-Sea Museum)

In old Leigh, the sea swept through the cockle sheds and along the High Street to a depth of 3 feet. A bedridden lady of 94 was taken to hospital by police – for safety, while at nearby Two Tree Island, two men marooned on the roof of the sewage works were rescued by Leigh fishermen.

At 1.30 a.m. the Canvey partygoers were home when the tide peaked at 7 feet above the predicted level. In Peter Pan's playground, at the street end of the pier, the water was 8½ feet deep.

Low-lying Canvey Island is visible from parts of Southend, but that Sunday morning, nothing but the tops of houses and trees could be seen above the water. Southend immediately came to the aid of her neighbour. Boats of all kinds were assembled by the police from Southend, Leigh and other riverside towns. A miniature armada sailed to the rescue.

Ken Bolby, with other Leigh fishermen, set out at first light and worked all day Sunday, rescuing people from the most dangerous and inaccessible area – collecting them from the sea wall at Small Gains Creek and taking them to Bell Wharf in Leigh. Once safely there, a convoy of cars transported the cold and wet survivors to St Clements Hall, where tea, hot food and clothes were freely given.

Leigh fishermen, in their flat-bottom boats, were invaluable in the house-to-house search for survivors and bodies on Canvey. Ken Dolby remembered floodwater 5 feet deep in the bungalows on Sunday evening. On the following Monday, the gallant band of men were found rescuing people from Foulness.

The Southend lifeboat, *The Greater London Civil Service*, was called out five times on Saturday, then at 12.45 a.m., knowing the vulnerability of Canvey, she was launched, uncalled for, into rough seas to see how things were on the island. Diverted to ships in distress before reaching Canvey, the crew returned later to assist in rescue operations.

There were two fatalities in Southend due to the flood. An elderly man, Henry Ashwood, died of shock caused by getting out of bed into cold seawater and William Glover, aged 65, from Victoria Road, had been suffering from bronchopneumonia for a week and died on 8 February, as a result of immersion in water.

18

CANVEY ISLAND
AND BENFLEET

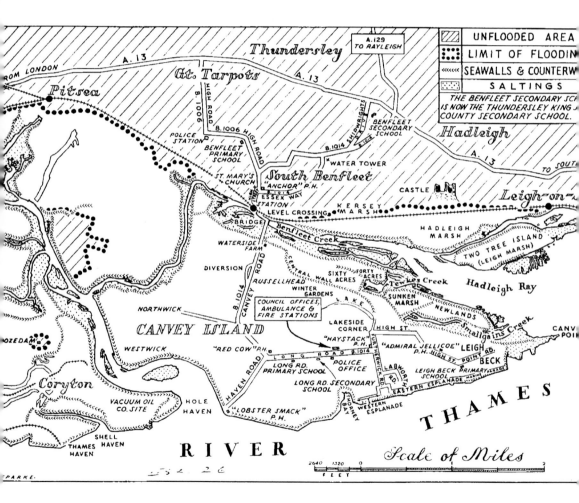

A map of Canvey Island in 1953. (Reproduced from the 1953
Ordnance Survey Map courtesy of Essex Record Office)

Canvey Island lies on salt marsh, which, over centuries, has been claimed and reclaimed by successive landowners whose new walls restrained the sea. Old walls (known as counter walls) remain standing and are visible today as grassy banks. Canvey High Road is sited on an old sea wall. In 1953, the wall facing the mainland was of earthwork, with a height of 5 feet above the highest tide levels, while the wall on the south of the island had a stone block face and was 1 foot higher. The whole island is lower than the level of spring tides. In 1953, one road and a narrow bridge connected Canvey to the mainland.

On the afternoon of Saturday, 31 January, Canvey's new War Memorial Hall was opened with a dance and social gathering. MP Mr Bernard Braine spoke briefly of the war years and said of the new hall, 'It will remind us that we are never so great as in adversity'.

As he was speaking, the North Sea surge, a wall of water nearly 10 feet above the predicted height of the spring tide, was roaring down the east coast and into the Thames estuary. Reduced in height, if not in speed or power, it approached Canvey with even greater adversity in its wake. When people left the hall to struggle home against the wind, the island was alone on the coast of Essex in knowing nothing of the impending disaster.

At 11.50 p.m. that night the Essex River Board Divisional Engineer telephoned Canvey Urban District Councillor Frederick Leach, of Waterside Farm, to warn him of an abnormal tide.

Mr Leach dashed straight to the bridge and found seawater splashing over from Benfleet Creek and beginning to creep down the road. He ran back home and rang Canvey police, before contacting a sea wall commissioner, who in turn called out two wall walkers. Mr Leach's call was the first news the police had received and they acted immediately by waking up Mr Reg Stevens, the County Surveyor and Engineer. At 12.05 a.m., Mr Leach and the bridge attendant erected flood boards across the road at each end of the bridge. Soon after this, the sea burst over, flooding the main road and surrounding farmland.

Albert Lynch and Roland Day were members of a team of nine on Canvey employed by the Essex River Board to inspect and report on the condition of about a mile of sea wall once a month. Albert and 'Rolly' worked on the wall at Tewkes Creek and, on being called out that night, inspected their section. Albert recorded in his wall walkers' notebook that water was beginning to spill over the wall at Tewkes Creek at 11.45. He then dashed the few yards to his house in Tewkes Road to warn his wife there would be a freak tide. 'It's coming over,' he shouted.

His son Derek, aged 20, returned from a dance and found his mother 'in a bit of a panic'. She said, 'Dad's been called out. There's going to be a freak tide – put old clothes on and go and get Nan and the dog from next door.'

Derek did as he was told and soon the family were crowded into the small room in the attic. He later recalled:

' I then went downstairs to make a cup of tea in the scullery out the back. Water was coming through floorboards, lifting the lino. I could hear water running and I thought I'd left the tap on. I looked at the back door. Water was pouring in through the keyhole! I knew then how deep the flood was outside. Then the door burst off its hinges. I ran upstairs and with the rest of the family watched the water rise to the top step. From our attic window all we could see was a huge lake of water. '

Derek's father, back on the sea wall, saw the first breech occur, taking away an area of wall 30 feet wide. At Small Gains Creek at the same time, Brian Brindle was securing his boat and thought the tide had turned when the water level dropped. But the drop had been caused by a breach on the other side of the creek, and seawater was rushing into the Newlands area.

Roland Day, standing on the wall, heard a terrific roar as the sea burst through a section opposite his bungalow in Munsterburg Road. Mr Day had left both his doors open so that floodwater, like an unwanted visitor, flowed through his home. The time was 1.30 a.m.

In the Lynch house, when the water receded, Derek kicked a door off its hinges and, with great ingenuity, made a bridge from the stairs to the window and climbed out into Roland's dinghy. His story continues:

The corner of Warden Road, Canvey in 1953. W.H. Williams, builder, would hope to sell plenty of his Wallpaper, Glass and Cement after the flood. (Mirrorpix)

' There was no one about. No sign of my father, who had gone down the road, waking people. As we rowed towards the sea wall we saw people on top of a roof and rowed across; there was a man, his wife, two small children and a baby. The woman passed the children down into the boat and climbed down herself. They were all wringing wet. We took them to the sea wall and went back for the man. It seemed to me that the baby was already dead. '

Wall walker Albert Lynch waded through the water, knocking hard on each door as he went. The area was a network of unmade roads and scattered bungalows, once familiar territory but now almost totally changed in the pitch darkness, and nearly impossible to navigate due to half-hidden debris. When the water reached his neck he climbed onto a veranda, where he was trapped for the rest of the night. Later, he told how heartbreaking it had been to hear children screaming and to have been unable to help. Within the house he saw an old man on a table and a woman on a wardrobe. Later, he heard that the wardrobe collapsed and the woman drowned.

The brother of 60-year-old Hannah O'Donoghue reported how, on 3 February, he entered his mother's house in Landsberg Road by breaking a window and found the body of his sister trapped under a fallen wardrobe.

By 1 a.m. Canvey was waking up. Most residents lived in two- or three-roomed bungalows, some had a small loft, the steps to which, to save living space, were often outside. Many islanders awoke when ice-cold seawater burst through their doors and windows to lap around their beds. Others slept on towards death.

The County Surveyor, Mr R.H. Stevens, had just retired to bed with the flu when the police knocked at the door shortly after midnight. He immediately left his home and 'went to the main sea wall, and in the moonlight saw a black menacing sea, calm, as the wind was offshore, and only about 12 inches from the top of the wall.' The surveyor was aware of the vulnerability of the low-lying north of the island and set off to investigate, en route making phone calls at the Council Offices in Long Road. He contacted his deputy, Dick Foyster, who, within half an hour, had alerted the fire brigade, ambulances and a doctor, and had arranged for schools to be opened as rest centres.

Reg Stevens drove to Haystack corner, where he left the car and walked to the High Street in water slowly flowing southwards. In the High Street the water was 2 feet deep and flowing so strongly that the constable on night duty, PC Bill Pilgrim, was hanging onto a lamp post. The surveyor joined him, marooned by seawater in which all manner of horrific debris was travelling.

Eventually, with a few local men, Stevens got to Small Gains Corner and broke into Prout's boatyard, carried a couple of boats to the High Street end of Chamberlain Road and paddled them towards Newlands. In the pale moonlight they could see the southern part of the Sunken Marsh area and, though the sea level outside the main sea wall had receded, inside it was to the top of the counter wall. The whole area resembled

Servicemen and civilians toiling to repair the sea wall at Tewkes Creek.
(Reuter's image, reproduced courtesy of Essex Record Office)

a saucer full of water up to 14 feet deep in places. A group of firemen could be seen wading through the water in a current so strong they had to link arms to cross the road.

By 7 a.m. Stevens got to the north side of the area, where people could be seen on roofs; heads could be seen emerging from holes in roofs and in some, known to be occupied, there was no sign of life. Two young boys recall being on a roof that night. Doug Neal lived in Winter Gardens:

' Dad got us into the loft and smashed a hole in the roof with a hammer, big enough for us to get out onto the roof. But the wind was so strong he was worried that we would be blown off. Someone had left a metal trunk in the loft; inside there were some puttees, the sort that First World War soldiers lashed round the tops of their boots. Dad used these to tie us to the chimney where we spent the rest of the night.

The following morning, rescued and sitting in a rowing boat, I asked, 'Mummy what's that in the apple tree?' to which she replied, 'Oh it's just some old clothes darling'. It was in fact a body. I remember being carried along a sea wall to a very warm houseboat and being given hot soup. And I remember being on a coach which took us to Benfleet. The family were in pyjamas and dressing gowns, with nowhere to go. '

Brian Winter remembered his parents wading through neck-high water when they left their flooded bungalow in Nevada Road; he on his father's shoulders and his sister on her mother's. A neighbour shouted for them to climb onto his roof and once there, with water now lapping against the guttering, they all sat hugging the warm chimney until rescued by police boat twelve hours later.

Some children perished as a result of the long wait on a roof. Twelve-year-old Leonard Starling's father wrote of the dreadful night he lost both son and wife: 'We were all in the house together on the night. At about 2 a.m. on Sunday the sea swept into my bungalow, and I got my wife and family onto the roof. We were taken off the roof by boats and were taken to some houseboats, where we became separated. I was later taken to a rest centre and did not see my wife and son again.'

Water was still flowing fast by Fletcher's shop on Sunday afternoon.
(Reuter's image, reproduced courtesy of Essex Record Office)

Both bodies were found on 2 February during rescue operations. No record has so far emerged as to precisely where they were found, or whether they made it to the houseboat. Twelve-year-old Leonard was drowned. His mother's body showed no evidence of drowning. She had sustained an injury to her spinal cord.

Peggy Morgan was also amongst those desperately shouting for help. At midnight, Peggy, her husband Reg and 5-year-old son Dennis were asleep in their bungalow in Adelsburg Road, but one hour later Peggy turned over in bed and plunged her arm into icy cold water. She shook her husband awake, and in the darkness they struggled through floating furniture to reach the sleeping child in the next room. Their one thought was to get out. Outside the water was waist high and rising. Clinging together, the family fought their way to their chicken shed and Reg pushed Peggy and Dennis onto the roof.

Reg's 74-year-old mother could be heard screaming from the bungalow next door. Her son struggled through the swirling water again to bring the terrified old lady to the shed, but, unable to climb up, she stood in the water holding Peggy's hand until the cold loosened her grip and she silently slipped away. Reg, already so numb with cold he could not speak, dropped under the water to try to find her. Neither was seen alive again.

Peggy and Dennis sat huddled together in the bitter cold for hours while dead animals, earth toilets and sheds crashed by them. Peggy never forgot the smell. She could hear people shouting for help, and eventually the lights of rescue boats appeared in the darkness. Later, there were no more boats and it became eerily silent except for the howling wind and the crash of doors and windows as the sea pounded them open. Peggy thought they had been forgotten. As they clung together, Dennis, in words that would haunt Peggy all her life, cried again and again, 'Mummy I'm so cold,' and her reply was always, 'I know darling, I'm trying to keep you warm.'

Peggy Morgan and five-year-old Dennis, who died in the flood on Canvey. (Courtesy of Stephen Champion)

When all hope was lost Mickey Saunders found and rescued mother and child. Now naked, their nightclothes ripped from their bodies by the waves and debris rushing by, they were helped into his dinghy, covered with a tarpaulin, and taken in an army lorry to the Long Road School. Mrs McCave, President of the Canvey WVS, recorded Peggy's presence at the rest centre and wrote in her report: 'There was a St John's nurse, in her arms a dying child, the mother having her cut legs dressed, the father had been drowned trying to save the grandmother'.

The above was written in hindsight. When Peggy was in the rest centre her husband and mother-in-law were missing. Phoebe Morgan's body was recovered three days later, and Reginald Morgan's after five days.

Peggy photographed in a rescue centre after her husband and son had drowned. (Courtesy of *Southend Standard*)

Five-year-old Dennis lived through that dreadful ordeal and showed signs of life on arrival at Southend General Hospital. He was given artificial respiration, oxygen, heat and stimulants, but all too late. He died of shock and exposure on 1 February.

In the hospital Peggy was told that her child was 'doing well' on the children's ward. When she was discharged a week later a priest was asked to break the news of her son's death.

Margaret Blagdon lived in the same small road as Peggy. On Sunday she was listed as safe at the rest centre and this appeared to be confirmed when a group of Quakers on search patrol rowed up to her home. The front door was open and the house flooded, but unoccupied. Unfortunately, 71-year-old-Margaret had left her home and was swept away by the flood. Her body was found floating, some distance away, on Tuesday.

The Reverend Father Bernard Manning, from the Catholic church, was out on a sick call in the Newlands area when he heard the roar of the sea wall giving way. He left his car and walked to Lakeside Corner, which he knew to be very low:

' On the way I met Mr Stevens, who had formed a clear picture of the disaster. At Lakeside I found water rising very quickly. With a young fellow, I waded to each house and, finding women and children sitting on ceiling rafters, carried them to safety. Several people whose homes we couldn't reach we knew must be dead. As daylight came we went to check the homes of all old people. From the first to the third we rescued people, but after that it was recovering the dead. '

Jean Lavermore heard from her parents that their friends Mr and Mrs Fuller were amongst those visited by the priest that night. Mr Fuller was recovering from an operation and when Father Manning brought a boat to their house, neither could get out of the window into it. They told him to leave them together. Katherine Fuller, aged 66, and her husband William, 68, drowned. They are buried at Cemetery Corner, Benfleet.

Stella Donoghue's grandparents, Fred and Dorothy Taylor, spent the whole night on top of a water tank, clinging to the house guttering. On 8 February 1953, Fred wrote a moving account of the night to their daughter Ivy. He described how below their slippery perch, 'the sea roared, seethed and boiled. Gradually the cries for help died away and one by one the lights in the bungalows went out.' When the tide receded, the exhausted couple managed to get indoors. Within a short time Mr Taylor set out to wade to his mother-in-law's house. At the bottom of the garden he was in water up to his neck and

The Sunken Marsh, Canvey Island, from above Tewkes Creek. It is worth noting that the first aerial photographs were taken on the afternoon of Monday 2 February. (Reuter's image, reproduced courtesy of Essex Record Office)

three soldiers pulled him out onto the wall. The incoming tide made it impossible to continue. His mother-in-law, 78-year-old Mrs Harriet Coates, and her 56-year-old son, William, were drowned in their home.

The situation on Canvey was desperate throughout the night. The walls around the island suffered 120 separate breaches leaving most of the land flooded. Where water was trapped within walls and counter walls it was between 8 and 14 feet deep. Rescue work was begun by firemen and other local people but was handicapped by lack of boats. Individual and group initiative was the key to the successful rescue operation, especially in the early hours. There were many heroic deeds. Nobody waited for instructions. The police later acknowledged the support they had received from members of the public and from other services. The Canvey sergeant reported, 'I know of no instance where it was necessary for a police officer to ask for assistance.'

The surveyor called – using the new radio transmitter – for rescue vehicles, boats, ambulances and the welfare services to be assembled at Benfleet to receive evacuees. Very soon the operation was being conducted on military lines, with fire and police reinforcements coming in. Rescue operations proceeded at a faster rate when twelve Leigh-on-Sea cockle bawleys arrived with the dawn. Soon, 150 refugees from Canvey had landed at Leigh. The Southend pleasure boats also rescued victims.

Mr Rumble, Clerk to Canvey Council, had organised rest centres in Canvey schools and before 2 a.m. fireman Frank Griffiths, unable to find the Leigh Beck School caretaker's address, broke the school padlock with an axe and began ringing the hand bell to awaken residents. Long Road School was opened next and the WVS and St John Ambulance staff, under the direction of Mr Mason, cared for refugees until floodwater entered both schools. The rescued (still in their wet clothes), along with helpers, were then taken to Benfleet Primary School on the mainland, which was opened at 4 a.m.

Canvey Island was home to some very resourceful and stoic old ladies who waited alone in their bungalows for rescue. Three elderly residents were woken soon after midnight. Eighty-year-old Mrs Wilson of Oxford Road had been to a wedding that day and was woken by a neighbour calling, 'Get up! Get up! Tewkes Creek wall has broken open.' Mrs Wilson recalls, 'The water was rising, then the mats began to swim, then the footstool started to dance over along with two chairs'. She climbed onto a table and sat there, cold but resolute, till rescue came at midday.

Mrs Lawrence woke to find water bubbling under the door. Within minutes it was waist high. She fell into the water three times before managing to climb onto a washstand, where the depth of water forced her to stand in a stooping position, with her head touching the ceiling. There she stood, shivering with intense cold, until 2 p.m. on Sunday, when an AA Patrol Inspector, Mr H.T. Coy, and his assistant Mr Dennison helped rescue her from her home. They were called to Canvey at 11.30 a.m. Sunday and worked with firemen keeping the roads clear for the lorries needed to transport victims to the mainland. In between they joined rescue crews. Mrs Lawrence was heard calling from her bungalow,

John Wright's home behind the lorry in Mornington Road. John had been standing on the veranda fending off sheds and heavy timber in the fast flowing water which threatened to crash into the bungalow. (Mirrorpix)

but the men were unable to get in until, using their commandeered boat as a battering ram, with one man on the boat and the other holding onto the veranda upright, they used a synchronised see-saw action with the boat and eventually broke down the door.

Mrs Lawrence was taken to the High Street where, barefooted and wearing only her knickers, vest and a plastic mack, she walked to Furtherwick Road. The old lady was taken to Benfleet Primary School in the back of an open lorry and given some clothing.

A private car then transferred her to Benfleet Station, and, taking advantage of the free rail travel offered to Canvey residents, she made her way to Leyton. Finally, with no money or belongings, she walked to her sister's house. Like many Canvey evacuees, Mrs Lawrence landed unannounced on the doorstep of a relative who knew nothing of the flood. She later said of herself: 'Broken in body and spirit, I felt I had lost all that I'd worked and saved for all my life,' but within months, thanks to the Lord Mayor's Relief

Fund, her house was refurbished and the old lady was photographed standing at her door, smiling broadly.

Seventy-year-old Mrs Florence Rudge of Berg Avenue sat in her flooded kitchen for fifty-two hours until, on Tuesday, 3 February, she was the last person to be rescued.

Interviewed by MP Bernard Braine for the BBC in 1953, the feisty old lady told how she had been woken by water soaking her bedclothes:

‘ There was only one thing for it – I jumped onto this table that was floating round the room and there I stood until late Sunday. Yes late Sunday! It was about five o'clock. I was so exhausted by standing I slipped down and sat on the table with my legs in the water. I sat like that until I was rescued. I had a nice little bottle of whisky my daughter had brought back from Ireland, but that was in the bedroom; well I couldn't get it so I had nothing at all until they took me to hospital. I kept losing myself but I knew I had to keep my senses otherwise I would have gone into the water. I fought against sleep and I fought against unconsciousness but don't think I could have lasted another night. ’

Mrs Rudge rescued at last! (Courtesy of Southend-on-Sea Museum)

With little hope of survival, without food, water or sleep, her indomitable spirit kept her alive until she was carried to a boat and taken to Southend Hospital.

A spokesman reported that 'although in a distressed condition when rescued, Mrs Rudge quickly recovered and was soon back living in her home'. Mrs Rudge later told the MP, 'Old Hitler couldn't beat me and the sea wasn't going to!'

Before dawn, in the Sunken Marsh area, Kars Pruin, afterwards known as 'the mad Dutchman' for the tremendous and selfless rescue work he undertook that night, left his houseboat *Tideways*, moored in Tewkes Creek, and pulled a small boat over the sea wall. He launched out among the submerged bungalows, rescued people from their homes and helped them along the wall to his houseboat, where his wife, Gertrude, waited with warmth and hot soup. Soon, forty people were sheltering on the boat. Some were injured and two were holding dead children in their arms.

A Scottish welding inspector, Mr Robertson, assisting Mr Pruin, heard a baby crying in a pram on the veranda of a bungalow. While the Dutchman held the boat steady against the garden fence, the welding inspector climbed out and waded through 5 feet of water to the bungalow. A man's body, later identified as the baby's father, 30-year-old Ernest Foster, was found hanging over the veranda, and though the inspector searched and called through the bungalow, he found no trace of the mother. He took the baby out of the pram, carried it through the water to the boat, wrapped in his jacket, and rowed back to the houseboat.

The 'flood baby' has become legendary. The most common version of the story tells of the baby found floating, alone, far away from the bungalow in a Moses basket, twelve hours after the first flooding. Eight-week-old baby Linda, orphaned but otherwise unharmed, was brought up by her maternal grandparents.

Linda's 29-year-old mother, Elsie Foster, lived and died at her home 'Charma' on Athos Avenue. Elsie's father identified her body and stated that 'at about 1 p.m. on 4 February I went to Charma and found water all around it. I saw a body lying on the veranda at the side of the bungalow, under the baby's pram. The body was naked and the only means of identification was a brown mole in the corner of her right eye. It was my daughter. I handed the body over to the police who were working in that area in a boat.' The survival of the baby was a symbol of hope at a time of tragedy.

When the general water level decreased, roads built on old counter walls, though still under water, were high enough to allow the passage of traffic, and young islanders like Brian Lara of Larup Avenue volunteered to help the rescuers. He spent eight hours with Army personnel, driving around the island, guiding them along invisible roads to outlying bungalows and waiting in the cab while people were carried from their homes.

By midday on Sunday, water was still trapped in places and people still marooned in their homes. Half-hidden obstacles hampered progress of boats, and foot-rescuers risked stumbling off paths into cold and dirty water up to their armpits. Many people made their own way to dry land. A note was made at Dark Lane School rescue centre of a woman having pushed a pram from Canvey to the mainland with five small children. Her baby had to be thawed out by the kitchen stove. One man poled himself along in a dustbin until the bottom fell out. A pregnant woman was rescued by her husband by means of a tin bath, which he grabbed as it drifted by.

One mother's bravery saved her entire family. Mrs Doris Proops woke at 2 a.m. and grabbed her 9-month-old boy from his cot and her two daughters, aged 5 and 11, from other bedrooms. Her husband climbed onto a windowsill and held the baby. Mrs Proops put the younger girl onto a sewing machine, the only thing not floating, while the older girl stood up to her shoulders in water. Realising their chances of survival were practically nil, the mother dropped out through a window into the flood to swim to Central Wall, 25 yards away, but the current was too strong and the cold so intense that she returned to the house, swam round the back and climbed the ladder to the loft. There she found a blanket, which she tore into strips to make a rope and let down to her husband 10 feet below. He tied the baby to the rope and she hauled the child to the loft window. The two other children and her husband were pulled to safety the same way.

The Canvey Baptist minister Mr Hodgson, along with John Nesbitt from the Salvation Army, assisted by carrying children and the elderly to waiting lorries and ambulances.

Mr Liddiard found a way to get through the floodwater. (canveyisland.org)

One woman in a lorry, exhausted, clad only in a nightdress and flimsy dressing gown, said she had lost her little girl, who was drowned. The woman sitting next to her was carrying a fur coat, which she put around the shivering woman and told her to keep. The little girl who drowned was 4-year-old Julia Goodman of Hadleigh View, Komberg Crescent. Both her parents were taken to Southend Hospital. The following day, the two men helped search and mark houseboats and to label and carry the dead to lorries on the High Street.

Alice Davidson died trying to save her dogs. (Courtesy of Maree Klingsick. Photograph restoration by Barny Photography, Benfleet)

Shirley Thomas and her family awoke like so many others that night to see water outside the bungalow almost to the top of the window. Their father decided to sit them all on the roof rafters, where they spent the rest of the night, terrified of dozing and falling into the water below.

In another bungalow in Somnes Avenue, 5-year-old Keith probably fell asleep on the rafters in his home and despite the heroic effort of Chris, his 13-year-old brother, he did not survive. Later, their father told the tragic story of what happened to his family that night:

' At about 12.30 a.m. on Sunday, 1 February, I was awakened by my dog barking. We got up and my wife and I found that the bungalow was flooded to about 2 feet. I made a hole in the ceiling and with the aid of a table started to get my nine into the loft. I got seven up there and the table gave way, leaving my wife standing in the water with the other two children in her arms. At about 8 a.m. that day Keith fell through the hole in the ceiling into the water and another of my sons dived in after him and tried to hold him up. By this time the water had reached about 5 feet. After about two hours my son's strength gave way and he had to let go of Keith and hang onto the edge of the top of the door. He remained there until we were rescued by boat. My other two sons died in my wife's arms. '

Keith would have been 6 in two weeks; Gordon was 4 and Alan was 2.

Eventually, when rescue came, Chris carried out the body of his brother, and his mother held the bodies of her little boys. Almost naked, the remaining children were dried and dressed by local people and the family were taken to the Benfleet Primary School centre. Having lost three children and all they possessed, there was nothing for the family to do but find a corner of the crowded school.

Hugh Briggs of the County Welfare department, in charge of the school, reported on the first day that there was hardly room to move, but the centre was soon running smoothly, and hundreds of soaked and distressed refugees 'passed through'. Shirley Thomas and her sister, rescued before their parents and alone at the school, were not

The Queen Mother and Princess Margaret visit the centre at Benfleet Primary School. (Mirrorpix)

told to register on arrival and were housed with local people before their parents were rescued. Their mother was taken to hospital and their frantic father, with no record of his daughters' sojourn at the school, searched for three days, fearing they had drowned until, by chance, someone remembered them and they were traced.

Mr Briggs recorded that the first thought of all who reached the school was, 'Got a cup of tea luv?' But first they were able to choose from the clothing collected by the WVS and get out of their wet garments. A sense of humour was not lacking. When one of the workers called for soap powder the lady in charge, Mrs McCave, who had herself been evacuated from her home on Canvey during the night, waved a soup ladle as a weapon and shouted, 'If anyone mentions Tide, I'll brain them!'

On 3 February, the Queen Mother and Princess Margaret visited the primary school and, according to Mr Griggs, 'gave these poor folks a boost'. Children also got a boost from 12 tons of sweets donated by well-wishers, which were delivered during the first three days.

Thomas Flight and his wife were taken to the rest centre at King John School when rescued. The new school in Shipwrights Drive, due to be opened that week, was known locally as 'The Palace'. Mr Flight of Maybriar in Stanley Road described the night of the flood in a letter to his niece. His words epitomise the strength and stoicism of people caught in a disaster, who took everything in their stride:

> A fierce cold north wind had blown all day on Saturday. It was a new moon and the wind heaped up the water, which would normally have been a spring tide, into something like the Bore on the River Severn. About 1.30 a.m. a neighbour smashed at our door and cried 'Get up, the walls have collapsed'. We hurriedly dressed; the water was 3 feet 6 inches deep in no time. We have an upstairs attic but the stairs are outside. The pressure of water on the outer door was so great that the lock wouldn't turn. I had to break it off with a hammer. I shall never forget the shock as the door flew open and the icy cold water poured in with overwhelming force. We struggled upstairs somehow and watched the water steadily rise. It was a surging torrent; all manner of things were carried by it, including a caravan, any amount of heavy timber and several water tanks. The whole lot seemed to swirl as the wind and water acted, knocking against the wall and doors like battering rams. The water rose to about 7 feet on my ground.
>
> All night long we could hear people and children screaming for help, but nothing could be done till daylight. We personally shivered and chatted all night. I have never been so cold in my life.
>
> The military were soon giving most valuable help, and at about 10.30 on Sunday morning some of them, and a policeman, all covered with mud, took us off by boat. When we reached the wall at Gains Creek we were able to walk on the top, although in several places it was on the verge of collapse. Of course, we took nothing at all away,

except what we stood up in. I was unable to get my glasses even, but luckily we had our dentures. The soldiers were wonderful, most helpful and kindly. We were packed in a lorry. There were several poor devils in there almost naked, and men crying like children with their nerves all gone.

There were several centres; we were taken to a school at Benfleet, a wonderful place. They at once served us with hot tea and cereal and offered us a few dry clothes. I got a pair of flannel bags which finished halfway between my knees and ankles, but I was glad to put them on and take the wet bags off. We found that already people were offering to take survivors to friends and relatives in London. We were glad to accept.

We personally feel very grateful for the help and thankful that we escaped with our lives ... Uncle Hanson and Auntie Lottie next door were both drowned. **'**

'Uncle' Hanson Flight, aged 76, and his wife Charlotte, 72, lived in a wooden bungalow, 'Bankside', in Stanley Road. Their bodies were recovered by rescue workers five days after the flood. There was a tragic postscript to this story.

John Pinney, the grandson of Charlotte and Hanson Flight was at boarding school when, on 4 February, he read in the *Daily Mail* that his father had collapsed and died on the sea wall on Canvey. Mr Pinney, aged 47, coroner for East Ham and Walthamstow, had been given access to the Island to search, with his wife, for her parents. Tragically, the elderly couple were found drowned and, on hearing the news, John's father had a heart attack and died. John lost his father and grandparents within two days and learned of all the deaths by reading the newspaper.

At King John School thousands of refugees were fed and clothed for many days. Wilfred Pickles, the producer of the popular BBC's *Have a Go*, came to entertain and cheer them up.

Bill Gower has unusual but not unhappy memories of his time in the rest centre. His wife was heavily pregnant when their home was flooded. By laying a plank across a flooded ditch he helped her into their Dormobile and up to King John School. Bill then returned home for clothes.

The island was still flooded but Bill found a canoe with paddles in it, tied to a lamp post. He untied it and a soldier shouted out, 'Can I help you?' Bill explained and the soldier agreed to give him a hand. Bill continues the story:

' So we both got in this canoe and tried to paddle it down Furtherwick Road. I had no idea of how to paddle a canoe and neither had he and there was still a current running and we ended up in a bush. Eventually we got to the bungalow.

I collected some clothes and put them into the canoe with the soldier. He had got the idea of paddling by now and managed to manoeuvre across the deeper water. Then I had an idea. I got my wife's bike out of the shed and started pedalling through the water but when I got to this dip, for a few seconds I was cycling on water. Then the bike came to an abrupt halt and sank. I came off, right down into the water. When I came up my clothes were full of white worms and I had to go back in the water to get the bike. I chucked it over a neighbour's hedge.

Back at the school, a doctor sent my wife to Rochford Hospital and within a couple of days she had the baby. Now the *Southend Standard* and all the local papers reported that 'Mrs Gower had had the first flood baby'. Later, at the school, I had three blokes each trying to give me a brand spanking new pram. I said, 'Thanks but no thanks, we've already got one pram, we don't need three more. Why don't you give them to somebody here who needs them?' To this day I still don't know if Rodney was the first flood baby on the whole east coast. He certainly was the first from Canvey.

'

Four-year-old Heather Elliott managed to rescue her doll and brought it to the rest centre at Benfleet School. (Courtesy of Women's Royal Voluntary Service)

Seven-year-old Ian Nelson, sitting on the right with his brother. Ian's body was the last to be found on Canvey. (Courtesy of Maree Klingsick)

Five-year-old Maree Nelson and her family lived in May Avenue, close to their maternal grandparents, Mr and Mrs Davidson in Vadsoe Road. On the night of the flood, Maree's 7-year-old brother, Ian, was staying in Vadsoe Road with his grandparents.

Both houses were flooded but the ubiquitous Mr Pruin was quick to rescue Mr and Mrs Nelson and the six children, taking them from their bungalow to a waiting lorry, which took them to Benfleet School.

In the grandparent's house a tragedy occurred, the details of which are lost. Mr Davidson climbed onto a table and up into the loft. He later told his family that his wife refused to climb to safety and leave their two dogs to drown. There is no family memory of the mention of young Ian at this stage, or of what happened next in the bungalow.

The grandfather was rescued alone from his loft on 1 February and taken to King John School, about two miles from the primary school, where his daughter and grandchildren were. Six days later, on 7 February, the body of his 63-year-old wife, Alice, was recovered from floodwater in or near her home by the police. Her son-in-law, Douglas Nelson, identified the body on 8 February.

On 10 February, the Benfleet Primary School rest centre passed on a message to the island police that Ian Nelson, aged 7, had been reported missing. Police records state that no enquiry had been made earlier. As soon

The Nelson family repaired the bungalow where Ian and Alice died. (Courtesy of Maree Klingsick)

as the message was received the police found the child's body. His was the last body recovered from the island. Mr Nelson identified his son the next day. The body had been in the water for ten days. There remains no official record of where the two bodies were found, but family members believe that Mrs Davidson's body was recovered from the house, or just nearby, possibly entangled with a dog's lead round a lamp post, and Ian's was found between the palings under the bungalow.

Sixty people from the Sixty Acres and Winter Garden area were rescued by members of the South Benfleet Yacht Club. Ron Sewell, a retired detective Chief Inspector, reported on their superb work: 'They rowed their boats from South Benfleet and the eight male members rescued people in their boats and brought them to the inner sea wall, while the two women guided those who were strong along Central Wall Road, an inner sea wall, to safety, and the old and weak to an empty house where they had prepared fires and tea.'

Roger Gilbert, a member of the group, described how at one point a caravan floated past with a woman waving frantically from inside. After debating the pros and cons of opening the door, they eventually pulled her out of the window into their dinghy. Another woman recovering from an operation, with a stitched wound in her stomach, was rescued alone from her house, and, in lieu of a stretcher, Roger and the team dismantled the bed and carried her to the sea wall on the frame. Ron Sewell's report concludes,

A caravan floated by, with someone inside waving frantically. (Artwork by Mike Maynard)

Jones' Stores. (Courtesy of the Salt family)

'They carried out their self-appointed task in the face of a bitter wind and a strong current, which made their boats practically unmanageable, and they did not stop until they had made certain that every living person had been removed from the flooded bungalows. Had it not been for their efforts I am certain that the death toll would have been much greater.'

The Weston family were woken by their dog barking and found their home covered in rapidly rising water. Peter, aged 5, was lifted onto the table while his parents tried to break through into the roof space. But the table collapsed and all three went under the water. With no way of getting into the loft they stood with their heads just out of the water for hours. Peter could speak at first but after a while he 'appeared to go to sleep'. His parents held him until rescuers took the child away, returning later for the parents. Peter had died of heart failure due to exposure.

Very shortly afterwards, other youngsters were helping rescue and repair operations. On Canvey, as on other flooded localities, Sea Scouts, Rovers, Boy Scouts, Girl Guides and schoolchildren made tea and sandwiches, collected clothes, cleaned houses and filled sandbags. Val Long was 12 when she worked all night with the WVS, buttering bread for hundreds of sandwiches on a production line in Benfleet School.

A young Boy Scout was praised in a letter to senior Scouters:

'I was in charge of the men repairing breaches in the sea wall at Small Gains Creek, when three small lads came over the saltings to where we were filling sandbags. They asked me for a job and, because of their size, I detailed them to tying up filled sandbags. After a short while two of these lads went off elsewhere and the one who remained, Joseph Cotterel of the 4th Laindon Scout Troop, was carrying filled sandbags to the sea wall, a distance of some 20 yards, through knee-deep mud where fully grown men were finding it extremely hard going. When I told this lad not to do this heavy work, he promptly but respectfully told me he was a Boy Scout and had come prepared to work like the soldiers, because his training motto was 'Be Prepared'. Not wishing to hurt his pride I let him carry on for a while before again telling him to go back to tying sandbags, but he was not to be put off. He had no food or drink until I found him some at 4 p.m. and then he carried on until I had to practically force him to go home. The conditions were extremely bad for a lad so young. The deep mud and water made it extremely unpleasant. The Army called it 'Operation Bulldog'. I think this 'Bulldog pup' has truly earned the Scouts Silver Star for extreme devotion to the Scouts Promise.'

South Benfleet Sea Rangers received unexpected training in childcare when a local doctor and his wife opened their home to eighteen rescued babies. The 'mothercraft box' was opened and Girl Guides bathed, dressed and cared for the babies. The local chemist provided babies' bottles and nappies.

'Jones' Bear', outside the shop at Jones's Corner. The sign reads 'Bear up! Canvey will rise again'. (Courtesy of the Salt family)

Eight-year-old Chris Jennings was one of the few children who remained on Canvey throughout. Each day, abandoned animals were brought to the lounge of his home in the Jellico public house. Dogs, cats, rabbits, budgies and even a turkey were content to share the only available, and very crowded, temporary lodgings. Chris also remembered that his cat unexpectedly moved her newborn kittens from a downstairs cupboard to the top shelf of the airing cupboard on the morning of Saturday, 31 January, when the North Sea tsunami was a mere ripple in the waters of the Azores.

Canvey islander Mike Brown saw the flood from beginning to end. He wrote:

‘ When I was 20 I lived on a houseboat in Small Gains Creek with my parents. Having lived on a houseboat all my life I knew there would be an unusual tide that night and put out extra mooring ropes. We had a gangway leading to the boat which was always above high tide level, but by 9.30 that evening the tide had covered the gangway with a further two hours to high tide. By midnight the water level had reached the top of the sea wall and from the deck of our boat we could see right across Newlands.

Soon cries could be heard. My father could not swim so I insisted he stayed on the boat. In my waders I managed to cross our gangway to my 14-foot dingy and pull it over the sea wall. The scene of devastation was unbelievable and the screams and cries for help will be with me forever.

I rowed to the other side of Newlands, as I knew this was where the wall had been breached, and as I passed the bungalow on the corner of Brandenburg and Nordland Roads, I saw a man sitting on the roof. He would not get into my dinghy but asked me to look for his wife. I rowed round and saw a woman caught in a tree on the other side of the bungalow. She was obviously dead. I then rowed towards some cries for help and rescued a family of four from the roof of a bungalow in Hornsland Road. I took them to Small Gains sea wall, and because our houseboat was not accessible, they were taken in by another.

I went back to Newlands another four times and rescued eleven people in total, but, unfortunately, four died of exposure. By this time I was completely exhausted and my hands were bleeding from rowing. After a hot drink I decided to go back to pick up the man on the roof but he had died of exposure. I felt guilty that I had not been able to persuade him to get into my dinghy. When dawn broke all the cries for help had stopped; there was just an eerie silence. I wanted to sleep, but found I couldn't. All the emotions of that night then hit me.

The most upsetting thing for me was the body of the woman in her nightdress, that I found caught in a tree, was lying on the sea wall for two days with the press and other people walking round her. I found a tarpaulin and covered her. She was eventually taken to the front of Chambers Stores in the High Street with all the other bodies. ’

Corner of Brandenburg and Nordland Roads. Note the body on the roof and the watermark on the wall. (Shiner & Holmes image, reproduced courtesy of Essex Record Office)

Canvey resident Rod Bishop and others remember the bodies 'stacked up' at the side of Chambers Stores. A temporary mortuary had been arranged at the primary school in Long Road and between eight and ten bodies were taken there. Then, when the school was flooded, the police were given a council lorry for use as a mortuary, supplemented later by Stibbards, a local undertaker firm, and eventually handed over to them completely.

The suffering of those who found the bodies of relatives or were with them when they died is beyond measure. John Laverak and his wife lived in Edmonton but owned a house, 'Joy Nook', in Athos Avenue, where they were on 31 January. However, at 6 p.m. the next day Mrs Laverak turned up unexpectedly at her son's house in Edmonton, alone and very distressed. Their son went to Canvey the following morning to look for his father. He got to Athos Avenue in a boat and through a window in the bungalow saw his father floating face-down in 4 feet of water. He notified the police and at 10 a.m. on Wednesday the 4th, with two relatives, he recovered his father's body, took it to the top of Chamberlain Avenue and handed it over to the police who attached a label to his leg.

The Lloyd family experience is similarly heartrending. Brother and sister, Betty and Jack Lloyd, searched rest centres and hospitals in vain for their parents, John and Alice. Informed that all survivors had left the island and any remaining must be deceased, they finally persuaded the police to let them check for themselves. They found a boat and

PC Bill Pilgrim carries a child to safety from her flooded home on Canvey Island. (canveyisland.org)

punted their way to their parents' bungalow in Amid Road. Outside, they called out and heard their father's faint reply.

John later told how the water was waist high in the bungalow after six minutes and they got into the loft in their bedclothes. Alice, aged 79, died of shock within half an hour and her husband held her, while praying to die, until his family arrived on Monday.

Gertrude William's son was woken by the siren and went to his mother's bungalow. He saw that the water had risen above the windowsill. He too found his mother floating in the water. His brother-in-law and the military helped him recover the body.

Mr and Mrs Faiers and their 6-year-old daughter survived in their bungalow, clinging together from 2 a.m. until 1.30 p.m. when, tragically, 46-year-old Doris died. Her family were rescued just one hour later.

The devastation on Canvey was such that almost all residents were evacuated. Many families remained at 'The Palace' for two weeks; men going to work from there and children to school. Some dignitaries were in favour of abandoning Canvey to the sea, but the islanders thought otherwise. After a gargantuan effort by all volunteers and services, working day and night, cleaning and repairing homes and rebuilding walls, the people returned, and their beloved Canvey Island rose from the sea.

19

TILBURY

Tilbury lies on the north bank of the Thames, where the river narrows to approximately 800 yards. High tide was not due there until 1.58 a.m. on 1 February, but when the Tilbury Police Inspector was told of the Southend flood warning, he drove to the riverside with his sergeant to view the situation. Between Tilbury Fort and the ferry, they found the Thames flowing over the riverbank. The police officers roused the caretaker of Tilbury Fort and his wife and helped them through the water from their cottage to the nearby riverside pub The World's End. By 12.30 a.m., the flood had flowed inland 50 yards from the river wall – an occurrence never witnessed before.

The flooded centre of Tilbury town. (*Southend Standard*, reproduced courtesy of Essex Record Office)

A 1953 cartoon about the soldiers' HQ at The Red Cow public house – 'A soldier's farewell to Canvey'. (Reproduced courtesy of Essex Record Office)

Just after 1 a.m. the tide reached its peak at 9 feet above the predicted level. Water from the tidal basin began to flow into town. Ferry Road and Riverside Station were flooded, and there was 4 feet of water around the Tilbury and Riverside General Hospital. Built on higher ground, water never entered inside.

However, a second far more serious flooding developed when walls on the Tilbury marshes, to the east, were breached. A tremendous volume of water built up on the marshes and headed towards the town, joining the flow from breaches in Bill Meroy Creek and near Coalhouse Point.

Within minutes the whole of Tilbury, to the bottom of the hill at Chadwell St Mary, was flooded and water was halfway up the second storey of most houses. Residents Angela and Jim Rowland were woken at 3 a.m. by a neighbour warning them that water was coming across the fields: floodwater from the east, where it was least expected. The police and local volunteers began running through the streets, shouting and blowing whistles to wake people. Once upstairs, with whatever they could grab for comfort to take with them, people were trapped, unable even to flush their toilets as the sanitary services had failed. The Rowland family were rescued late on 1 February by servicemen wading through waist-high water to reach them. They were taken to an emergency centre at Chadwell St Mary School. The whole town was evacuated, most returning home by the end of February. There was one fatality in Tilbury; a 79-year-old lady died alone in her home. Trapped in her lavatory when floodwater entered the house, she was unable to force open the door.

Police Inspector Northover of Tilbury, in his report, praised the efforts of the services, hospital staff, and volunteers of all ages, especially Scouts, Cubs, and Brownies. He also commented that, 'The courage and cheerfulness of the people of Tilbury in the face of widespread disaster was really wonderful'.

WILL IT EVER
HAPPEN AGAIN?

King Canute, in the eleventh century, set his throne by the seashore to demonstrate (contrary to popular belief) that even a king could not command the waves. In 1950, the government set up Operation King Canute to provide fast response to any threat to the sea walls of Essex. On 1 February 1953, Operation King Canute, with Army and RAF personnel called swiftly to action, made headquarters at the Red Cow pub on the edge of the flood line on Canvey Island. Closing of the breaches began immediately. The pub,

The power of the sea. A flood-damaged house in Alexandra
Street. (Courtesy of Harwich Town Council)

Troops filling sandbags outside The Red Cow pub, soon to be renamed The King Canute. (Reuter image, reproduced courtesy of Essex Record Office)

with its name now the King Canute, is a reminder that the power of the sea can never be fully controlled by man. The east coast will never be free of the threat of flood, and man will continue the battle to keep the sea in its place. Since 1953, greatly improved flood warning systems and sea defences, plus the vigilance of the Anglian (Regional) Flood Defence Committee, allow us, at present, to sleep easy in our beds.

RECORDED DEATHS DUE TO THE FLOOD IN ESSEX

HARWICH

ALBERT STREET
Gladys Bruce, 23
Pauline Bruce, 16 months
Walter Mallows, 60

FERNLEA ROAD
Edward Ellis, 68

GRAFTON ROAD
Stanley Vincent, 53

STATION ROAD
Frederick Shipley, 74
Lilian Shipley, 63

STOUR ROAD, ANCHOR HOTEL
Pearl Lofts, 64

BRAMBLE ISLAND
Henry Archibald, 68 (of Little Oakley)

JAYWICK

BEACH CRESCENT
Jessie French, 77

CORNFLOWER ROAD
Ada Kendall, 62
Marie Miles, 42
Lucy Willson, 73
Samuel Willson, 71

FLOWERS WAY
Dorothy Hamilton-Ross, 71

GLEBE WAY
Florence Brookman, 70
Hilda Brookman, 36

GOLF GREEN ROAD
Edward Bishop, 79
Florence Bishop, 73
Florence Buckle, 67
Harry Buckle, 70
Kate Lacock, 78
Ernest Rogers, 65
Rose Saward, 45

MEADOW WAY
Helena Bangle, 62
Nellie Burnett, 69
Sarah Dempster, 61
Harriet Fox, 74
Esther Jew, 89
James Wm Jew, 86
James Jew, 60
James Ketley, 74
May Ketley, 68
Lavinia Lambert, 71
Herbert Law, 76
Margarita Law, 74
Maud Pym, 69
Emma Scott, 78
Florence Weatherburn, 69

SINGER AVENUE
> Joseph Brydson, 38
> Lillian Davill, 41
> Michael Davill, 11

TRIUMPH AVENUE
> Mary Ann Payne, 68
> Reginald Payne, 38

ST OSYTH

POINT CLEAR, CROSSWELL STORES
> Lilian Crosswell, 58
> William Crosswell, 58

FOULNESS

COURTS END
> Bertha Rawlings, 64

FISHERMAN'S HEAD
> Violet Rawlings, 41

KINGS HEAD PUBLIC HOUSE
> Captain F.A. Cook, 60

CREEKSEA

> Charles Rolfe, (from Rochford), 43

HAVENGORE

> Stanley Gray, (War Department
> Constable), 47

WALLASEA

> James Burns, 70

GREAT WAKERING

HOME FARM ESTATE
> Stuart Curtis, 3
> Ellen Kirby, 69

George Kirby, 71
David Whitehead, 4
Nellie Whitehead, 24

LANDWICK COTTAGES
> William Driscoll, 40

NEW ROAD
> Walter Manning, 67

SOUTHEND

BARNABY ROAD
> Henry Ashwood, 75

VICTORIA ROAD
> William Glover, 65

CANVEY ISLAND

ADELSBERG ROAD
> Margaret Blagdon, 71
> Dennis Morgan, 5
> Pheobe Morgan, 72
> Reginald Morgan, 37

AMID ROAD
> Alice Lloyd, 79

ATHOS ROAD
> John Laverak, 60

BRANDENBERG ROAD
> Alice Brooks, 81
> Daisy Deith, 68
> Ernest Deith, 70

CHURCH PARADE
> Elizabeth Jacobs, 69
> James Jacobs, 66
> Emily Price, 88

CORONA ROAD
> Emily Carter, 75
> Louisa LeMay, 63

CRAVEN AVENUE
Maria White, 65

DENHAM ROAD
Catherine Rawkins, 87

DEVENTER ROAD
Rebecca Keymer, 73

GILLS AVENUE
Rose Hindle, 68

HEESWICK ROAD
Harriet Coates, 78
William Coates, 56
Alice Farrow, 58

HEILSBERG ROAD
Alfred Hagan, 60
Mary Hagan, 62

JULIERS ROAD
Matilda Tearle, 66

KAMERWYCK AVENUE
Norah Dearman, 63

KELLINGTON ROAD
Doris Faiers, 46
Elsie Foster, 32
Ernest Foster, 30

KNIGHTSWICK ROAD
Katherine Fuller, 66
William Fuller, 68

KOMBERG CRESCENT
Judith Goodman, 4

LANDSBERG ROAD
Hannah O'Donoghue, 60

LARUP AVENUE
Julia Rennison, 76

MAY AVENUE
Ian Nelson, 7

MILTZIN AVENUE
Arthur Hobbs, 65
Agnes Simkins, 64

Caroline Smitges, 69

NEWLAND ROAD
Alice Smith, 74
Edith White, 60
William White, 62

NORLAND ROAD
Caroline Welham, 67

PARK ROAD
Alice Lloyd, 70

RAINBOW ROAD
Gertrude Wines, 68

SOMNES AVENUE
Alan Manser, 2
Gordon Manser, 4
Keith Manser, 5

STANLEY ROAD
Charlotte Flight, 72
Hanson Flight, 76

STRASBOURG ROAD
Peter Weston, 5

THE AVENUE
Arthur Fisher, 62

VADSOE ROAD
Alice Davidson, 63

WAALWYCK DRIVE
Edward Curtis, 83
Harriet Curtis, 83

WHERNSIDE AVENUE
Leonard Starling, 12
Violet Starling, 32
Gertrude Williams, 65

WITTEN ROAD
Elizabeth Collins, 74
James Collins, 74

TILBURY

unknown woman, 79

ABOUT THE AUTHOR

PATRICIA RENNOLDSON SMITH is a retired Headteacher and Ofsted Inspector. She has had articles published in the *Guardian* and has been interviewed on BBC Radio Essex concerning the East Coast Floods. Patricia (*née* Cleary) was a pupil at North Kensington Secondary School in Portobello Road, London in 1953 when news of the flood was announced in a school assembly, and a collection was made for the children of Canvey. She lives in Essex with her family.

BIBLIOGRAPHY

BOOKS

Barsby, Geoff, *Canvey Island: A Pictorial History*, Phillimore, 1992

Currie, I., Davison, M., and Ogley, B., *The Essex Weather Book*, Froglets, 2000

Hendy, Phyllis M., *Treacherous Tides*, Hendy, 2007

Grieve, Hilda, *The Great Tide*, Essex County Council, 1959

Harland, M.G. and H.J., *The Flooding of Eastern England*, Minimax, 1980

King, Carmel, *Without Warning: The Great Storm of 1953*, Ian Henry, 2004

Pollard, Michael, *North Sea Surge: Story of the East Coast Floods of 1953*, Dalton, 1978

Storey, Neil R., *Flood Alert!*, Sutton, 2003

Summers, Dorothy, *East Coast Floods*, David & Charles, 1978

Weaver, Leonard T., *The Harwich Story*, Harwich Printing Co., 1975

PRIMARY SOURCES

Essex Record Office 'Flood Files: 1953' were extensively used for research. ERO documents quoted from source:

    Mr Leonard (incl. Carter and Aynsley) C/D 11 Fd45/61

    Mrs Winchester. C/D 11 Fd45/72 (British Rail)

    Mrs Vivashi. C/D 11 Fd45/20 (British Red Cross)

    Mrs Symonds. C/D 11 Fd45/128

    Mr Serrell-Watts. C/D 11 Fd45/187

    Revd Father Manning. C/D 11 Fd45/87

    Boy Scouts Association. C/D 11 Fd45/54